Vital Signs

Anticipating, Preventing and Surviving a Crisis in a Nonprofit

by Melanie L. Herman
and Barbara B. Oliver

Copyright © 2001
by the Nonprofit Risk Management Center

ISBN No. 1-893210-06-5

**Nonprofit
Risk Management
Center**

Nonprofit Risk Management Center

The Nonprofit Risk Management Center is dedicated to helping community-serving nonprofits conserve assets, prevent harm, and free up resources for mission-critical activities. The Center provides technical assistance on risk management, liability, and insurance matters; publishes easy-to-use written resources; designs and delivers workshops and conferences; and offers competitively priced consulting services.

The Center is an independent nonprofit organization that doesn't sell insurance or endorse specific insurance providers. For more information on the products and services available from the Center, call (202) 785-3891, or visit our Web site at **www.nonprofitrisk.org**.

Nonprofit Risk Management Center
1001 Connecticut Avenue, NW
Suite 410
Washington, DC 20036
(202) 785-3891
Fax (202) 296-0349
www.nonprofitrisk.org

Staff

Sheryl Augustine, *Customer Service Representative*
Amy Michelle DeBaets, *Director of Management Information Systems*
Suzanne M. Hensell, *Director of Marketing and Education*
Melanie L. Herman, *Executive Director*
Barbara B. Oliver, *Senior Editor*
John C. Patterson, *Senior Program Director*

Public Entity Risk Institute

The Nonprofit Risk Management Center is grateful for the support of the Public Entity Risk Institute, which provided a generous loan to support the cost of publishing this book. PERI is a tax-exempt nonprofit whose mission is to serve public, private and nonprofit organizations as a dynamic, forward thinking resource for the practical enhancement of risk management. For more information on PERI, visit the organization's Web site at **www.riskinstitute.org**.

Acknowledgments

The authors are grateful to Mika Nakahara of Tokyo, Japan, for her invaluable research assistance during her fellowship with the Center. We are also grateful to the following persons for their thoughtful comments and helpful suggestions on the draft of this publication:

Louis B. Novick, *The Novick Group, Inc.*
Susan Sanow, *Washington Council of Agencies*
Mark D. Terman, *Kansas City Police Department*
Leslie T. White, *Croydon Consulting*

Table of Contents

Introduction

Headline news. Something nonprofits dream of having — when it showcases the nonprofit organization and its services in a positive light. Unfortunately, the news media thrive on tragedy, drama and scandal — not the good news. Crisis in the nonprofit sector feeds the frenzy, because the organizations are community-based and community-serving. What better way to pique the interest of readers, viewers and listeners than to run a story that gets them where they live and grabs their hearts. This book is designed to help you anticipate, prevent or survive a crisis in your agency.

Crisis management requires your investment of time and common sense, rather than a large budget. You do what you can, as you can, keeping the final goal of preserving your vital mission at the forefront. Consider your organization as a physician considers a patient. Check the vital signs to establish a baseline for future diagnosis. When you detect an aberration, determine the source, identify treatment methods, apply the methods and evaluate the results. Schedule regular checkups to monitor the organization's vital signs: the ones that enable the nonprofit to fulfill its mission by meeting critical community and client needs. This process will make a critical difference in your nonprofit's future health.

If your organization is healthy, determine what you can do to keep it that way long term. However, if you find that the nonprofit has several system weaknesses, you'll need to assess the symptoms, make a diagnosis and begin a treatment plan to cure what ails it so it can thrive or, at the very least, ease the symptoms to enable it to survive. Weaknesses might exist in the financial area, human resources, or volunteer management. The symptoms could manifest as uneven cash flow, a sharp increase in formal grievances, or a steep reduction in volunteer hours. The financial treatment plan could involve distributing major expenses throughout the year or asking past donors to increase their support. The human resources treatment plan might be to revise the staff and volunteer handbooks and provide training programs on expectations and procedures. The volunteer management plan would evaluate volunteer assignments in light of level of skills volunteers provide.

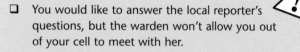

You Might Be Facing a Crisis if ...

❑ You would like to answer the local reporter's questions, but the warden won't allow you out of your cell to meet with her.

❑ The bank imposes an additional surcharge to print your statements in red ink to reflect your deficit balance.

❑ Your employees aren't sure where to report to work because your building no longer exists.

❑ When you arrive at the Grand Hotel for your nonprofit's annual meeting along with 500 of your members, you learn that a yodeling convention is in full swing and your contract is for next week.

❑ The bank manager calls to inform you that your business checking account is in arrears. The negative number she recites doesn't match the $200,000 balance appearing on the general ledger your trusted accountant gave you last Friday.

If possible, you'll want to make gradual changes, starting with the ones that will bring your nonprofit the most benefits, just as a sedentary patient with elevated blood pressure eases into lifestyle changes to bring the reading into a healthy range. You don't want the treatment to cause more damage than the disease. Instead of forcing a mountain of new policies and procedures on a staff accustomed to an informal work environment, which could send vital human resources running for the want ads, begin by looking at what works and what's missing.

As a leader who wants a healthier nonprofit, visualize what the organization would look like if it were strong and fortified to survive crises. Then divide and conquer the tasks required to reach your goal. How much less stressful this will be on you and your staff — and more do-able than laying down this book and thinking: OK, today I'm writing a crisis management plan and putting safety initiatives into practice and ... and ... and ... or the place will fall apart tomorrow. The critical difference between success and failure is how you approach crisis management. Ease into making your organization healthier and more likely to avoid a preventable crisis and survive the one fated to occur, or you and your staff risk burnout without completing the job.

Wise Investment

The time you spend daily on crisis management is a wise investment in the well-being of your nonprofit's future. Daily? Yes, daily. The secret is to schedule meetings, and assign tasks and due dates. A little bit here and a little bit there adds up to a whole lot. There are many steps you can take to stop crises from occurring.

Something as basic as integrating safety and risk reduction awareness into your organization's culture can make a huge difference. Staff who keep "slip, trip and fall" top-of-mind will secure that piece of loose carpeting without being asked to do so and before the elderly client steps on it. A volunteer who receives an oddly wrapped

Seven Essentials

If you only have limited time to spend on crisis prevention, use that time to get started on the following essentials for any nonprofit.

1. Create a comprehensive directory of the organization's staff, board and key volunteers. Include home addresses, phone/fax/wireless/beeper numbers, as well as emergency contact information. Distribute the list to employees and keep copies off site, as well as in your offices. Update and redistribute the list at least once a year.

2. Maintain a backup of your computer file server and key databases and financial files. Update the backup every week (at least) and store a copy off site or in a fireproof safe.

3. Store a copy of all insurance policies, vehicle and property titles, vehicle registrations and bank account numbers in a safe deposit box or fireproof safe.

4. Engage an independent accounting firm to perform a comprehensive annual financial statement audit. The auditor should report directly to the board at a regularly scheduled board meeting or at a special session called to discuss the audit findings.

5. Establish an ongoing relationship with an attorney familiar with your state laws whom you can call upon from time to time for advice and assistance. If your nonprofit doesn't have the resources to pay a monthly retainer or substantial hourly rate, consider soliciting bids from prominent law firms, emphasizing the charitable work of your agency. Don't be surprised if you receive proposals offering pro bono or dramatically discounted legal services.

6. Review emergency and crisis management procedures at least once a year with all staff and key volunteers. If you don't have procedures indicating "who does what" in the event of an emergency, make it a top priority to create them.

7. Update your written personnel policies and procedures every year and brief staff on the intent and content of these key policies. And when doing so, always KISS: Keep it simple, sweetie. The more voluminous your policies, the less likely it is that anyone (including supervisory staff) has read them. Give your handbook to individuals to whom an offer of employment has been made. Then, require that when individuals accept positions at your nonprofit, they also certify in writing that they have read and agree to abide by your policies. Provide an opportunity for any staff member to ask questions or seek clarification about your employment policies at least annually.

package, will alert the proper person who can determine if the contents contain a bomb.

Making certain that your personnel policies and procedures are clearly stated and understood by staff and volunteers will avoid responses of "I didn't know I couldn't wear short shorts to the jail" or "But, I was only visiting adult-oriented Web sites during my lunch hour!"

Acknowledging financial vulnerabilities will open the door to finding alternate funding sources, establishing a line of credit during good times and tailoring an insurance program to meet the needs of your nonprofit.

For the impetus you have no control over, things like natural disasters, arson or the board chair dropping dead the same day your executive director takes a new job, for these you need a crisis management plan. This plan would indicate who needs to be notified, who would run the organization, how clients would be served, what insurance covers, how to deal with the media, and everything else needed to fulfill the nonprofit's mission.

Now, let's get started. The first thing to do is to peruse this book.

Chapter 1
Symptoms of a Crisis

Throughout the 1990s, the phrase "crisis in a nonprofit" was often a euphemism for "scandal" as the media began focusing unprecedented attention on the misfortunes, mismanagement and outrageous fund-raising schemes of a handful of organizations. The decade ended with widespread apprehension about the implications of the "Y2K" issue: microchip-related disasters. Worldwide preparation paid off, and no catastrophic events were reported and attributed to the Y2K problem. The Y2K no-show provides an excellent example of the difficulty in measuring the value of preventing a crisis, and it's unlikely we'll ever know what disasters were averted through awareness and planning.

Crises are hardly confined to scandals involving top management or technology-inspired emergencies. The challenge for every nonprofit — from the smallest all-volunteer organization to the largest, multi-site social services agency — is to go one step beyond what happened in the past, and consider what might possibly go wrong in the future.

Crises can be brought on by human frailty or by natural fury, by wrongful acts or acts of God. A crisis can strike without warning or build over time. The sudden accidental death of a charismatic CEO or the theft of an organization's computer network file-server may catch everyone in an organization by surprise. In other cases, the seeds of a crisis are planted by the action or inaction of key personnel and germinate slowly. The warning signs, which should have been evident, may be obscured by the organization's ambitious service delivery, high turnover and complex fundraising efforts. In both cases, the nonprofit's paid staff and volunteer board may claim they "never saw it coming."

Defining Crisis

In 1996, the Nonprofit Risk Management Center published *Crisis Management for Nonprofit Organizations: Ten Steps for Survival.* In this book, we defined crisis as a sudden situation that threatens an organization's ability to survive: an emergency, a disaster, a catastrophe. We further stated that a crisis may involve:

- ❑ death or injury,
- ❑ lost access to the use of facilities and equipment,
- ❑ disrupted or significantly diminished operations,
- ❑ unprecedented information demands,
- ❑ intense media scrutiny, and
- ❑ irreparable damage to an agency's reputation.

The ability of an organization to continue functioning in the near future and survive in the long term is called into question because of a threat to one or more of its vital assets. A nonprofit's assets generally fall into one of the following categories:

1. people,
2. property,
3. income, or
4. reputation.

For nonprofit organizations, every decision takes on tremendous importance. Like a surgeon in the final stages of a dicey procedure, each move can either allow the patient to survive, be impaired or expire.

Threats to an organization's ability to achieve its mission threaten its essence. Vulnerable clients rely on the organization's services, employees need a paycheck, donors and sponsors have invested funds, and volunteers have devoted time and energy to a cause they believe is worthy. Managing a crisis in the nonprofit world is about more than just survival; it's about honoring commitments.

Origins of a Crisis

Nonprofit sector crises spring from familiar roots. An organization is likely to face a crisis whenever one of its clients suffers a serious injury or dies while participating in its programs. A crisis can occur when a nonprofit discovers the theft of a large sum of money. Or if a fire in a neighboring business engulfs the nonprofit's facility. While the root causes or precipitating events may be the same from one decade to the next, the technology of the "information age" has exacerbated the situation. The rapid dissemination of information (and misinformation) has increased the complexity of crises and the speed with which they can escalate.

For example, although every organization owning a computer in 1990 had reason to be concerned about data loss from power surges, equipment theft or hardware/software malfunctioning, few worried about the threat of a hacker disabling a Web site or a "worm" infecting the in-house file server. Few had contemplated the possibility of computer-based viruses spreading across the globe overnight by e-mail. Even as recently as five years ago, only a small percentage of nonprofits had Web sites. Today, countless organizations have Web sites (and some have ventured into the world of e-commerce) leaving clients open to the possibility of credit card theft or misuse and the nonprofit itself vulnerable to malicious attack.

As the old cliche states: The more things change, the more they stay the same. It's true that the range of potential sources of crisis have grown dramatically. However, the basic tenets of crisis management and the fundamental strategies for avoiding and surviving a crisis remain applicable, even in the information age.

For harried nonprofit executives and managers, it can be difficult sometimes to recognize a crisis when it occurs. This is especially true for the "creeping" crisis — one that sneaks up on us when our attention is elsewhere. Whether through a loss of vital funding, or a disappointing fund-raising drive, a financial crisis may not be realized until many months after the precipitating event. In the next chapter, we will examine the many forms that a crisis can take.

Chapter 2
Diagnosis of Nonprofit Crises

I n this chapter we will explore the various faces of crisis specific to a nonprofit organization. These issues distinguish the way a crisis may emerge and should be handled when a nonprofit — as opposed to a private business — is the victim or cause of a crisis.

Faces of Crisis

The descriptions of these nonprofit variations in crisis development and crisis management follow:

- **The Ties That Bind** — Every nonprofit is inextricably tied to other organizations, from its funders and constituent groups to client organizations. Thus, the source of a crisis facing a nonprofit may be another organization's disaster. For example, several years ago a number of District of Columbia nonprofits that provided services to the D.C. government were unable to meet basic operating expenses and the likelihood of bankruptcy loomed large. This crisis was, in large part, caused by the D.C. government's financial crisis and inability to pay its nonprofit contractors for services delivered.

- **Image Is Everything** — Reputation and image are like blood and oxygen to a nonprofit. Nonprofits rely on the impressions, opinions and goodwill of others, including clients, volunteers and funders. This dependence makes a nonprofit particularly vulnerable during a crisis when there's no way its reputation won't be called into question. The classic example is the United Way of America. The criminal actions of its 22-year president, William Aramony, and his conviction in 1995 not only disparaged United Way, but discredited and devalued the entire nonprofit sector. Names were sullied, funds were cut-off and it has taken the sector years to recover.

- **Public Accountability** — The public interest component of the nonprofit sector — a collection of organizations that serve a public interest — means that crises, as well as triumphs, will garner the attention of the public. The public is interested in what nonprofits claim to do, as well as their achievements and stumbles. This interest is necessary to the survival of most nonprofits. It can also cause an event of minor significance to mushroom into a crisis that attracts unfavorable media attention and threatens the organization's survival. Not long ago a story about the embezzlement of $1 million by an insurance company employee was buried on page 24 of an industry publication. No mention of the theft appeared in the mainstream media. A theft of that size occurring in a nonprofit organization would likely have drawn widespread coverage across the country.

■ **Inadequate Risk Financing** — Only a relatively small percentage of the more than 1.5 million nonprofits in the United States purchase any form of insurance. While insurance can't restore an organization's damaged reputation, it can ensure that funds will be available to replace damaged property, cover medical expenses and compensate victims of harm. Insurance is only one form of risk financing — access to a line of credit or adequate financial reserves are other strategies, but these are rare.

Types of Crises

Crisis management literature is replete with characterizations of crises. Understanding the impetus of a crisis can help you visualize how a crisis might develop in your organization and different crisis management strategies. In the following pages, we explore these characterizations and discuss their relevance to nonprofits.

Small Nonprofits

Crisis prevention is doubly important for small nonprofits. Why? Because small organizations often have less resources to draw on when a crisis erupts. And insurance and other risk financing tools may not be available due to the organization's meager financial resources. But every organization, from the smallest to the largest, can and should take steps to prevent the preventable and prepare for the unavoidable. Think of the advice in this book like a buffet — select the strategies that appeal to your organization and best suit your situation, but don't delay, because once you've undertaken some of these activities, you'll feel better knowing that your organization will be able to survive a crisis.

Seize Versus Squeeze

In their book, *Effective Crisis Management: Worldwide Principles and Practice,* authors Mike Seymour and Simon Moore draw a distinction between two major classes of crisis. The first is a crisis that strikes suddenly and without warning like the attack of a cobra. Using the authors' framework, certain natural disasters — floods, tornadoes, hurricanes, mudslides, hail storms — could be characterized as cobras. You can't prevent them, but you can be prepared to evacuate the building and provide services from another location.

The second major class of crisis "can steal up and gradually crush you, issue by issue," like the attack of a python. A major cultural and historical institution is among the nonprofits to feel the python's death grip. Over several decades, the financial condition at the organization reached crisis proportions due to various events and circumstances, including the nonprofit's acceptance of gifts that it could not afford to maintain and numerous ill-fated decisions by management and the board. A system of checks and balances could have helped prevent this crisis.

The moral of the snake analogy is that a crisis can develop with startling speed, paralyzing an organization and making it difficult to respond or recover. A nonprofit needs to be prepared for the type of crisis that strikes without warning, as well as the crisis whose grip tightens slowly and silently.

External Versus Internal

A natural disaster is an excellent example of a crisis from outside the organization. The action or inaction of a nonprofit can't cause a true natural disaster — a flood, tornado or earthquake — or prevent one from occurring, but natural disasters do affect nonprofits, keeping them from fulfilling their missions. Other external sources would include arson, random violence or a terrorist attack. While a crisis caused by external events or nature can't be prevented by a nonprofit, every organization should develop a strategy for responding to these events to protect people and property, and provide services. How an organization responds could make all the difference.

Many crises that strike nonprofits come from within, such as a lawsuit alleging employment discrimination or theft by the volunteer treasurer. It's important to attempt to do everything you can to prevent crises that come from within. Every nonprofit should identify internal actions that are potential sources of a crisis and take steps to minimize the likelihood of their occurrence.

Preventable and Unavoidable

A further way to distinguish or characterize a crisis is whether it was unavoidable or preventable. Although the cause of the crisis is easily distinguished, it isn't as easy to compartmentalize the necessary preparation, management and coping techniques. Just because an event (e.g., a tornado or flood) can't be prevented, doesn't mean that an organization should miss the opportunity to alter the effect the crisis will have on the organization. In the language of risk management, this is called mitigating a loss. For example, a flood may require a nonprofit to evacuate its premises. It may use whatever time is available to make certain that essential files are relocated to an alternate location, thus avoiding the need to recreate those files once the floodwaters have subsided.

Isolated or Linked

A crisis can affect a nonprofit in isolation, but few crises can be resolved effectively in isolation. For example, a lawsuit alleging racial discrimination is an event that affects a single organization. To prevent this event, which may be a crisis for some organizations, a nonprofit should develop thoughtful employment practices and take steps to administer them in a fair and consistent manner. To survive the suit, a nonprofit must obtain help from legal counsel.

Another form of crisis may involve several organizations. Consider the example (on page 9) of the crisis facing human service providers in the District of Columbia caused, in part, by the late payment of contract fees by the city government. To reduce the effect or avoid such an event, these providers needed to consider their relationships with others. For example, they might have asked, "How could our survival and good health be affected by our contract with the District of Columbia government?" They might have seen that a delay in contract payments by the city would keep them from meeting their financial obligations to staff and vendors and this, in turn, could jeopardize their survival. Some agencies might have pursued an underused risk financing strategy: bank financing in the form of a line of credit or an emergency short-term loan from a community foundation or funder. Or they might have contemplated another strategy, such as avoiding over-reliance on a government contract as the agency's principal funding source.

When a nonprofit's operations are inextricably linked to another, it must factor these relationships into the crisis management strategy. One way to do this is to form a crisis management team that includes individuals from several interconnected agencies. If a nonprofit's sole source of funding is a government agency, the crisis management and contingency planning effort might involve individuals from that agency.

A Specialized Form of Risk Management

Crisis management — a subset of risk management — focuses on enabling the organization to achieve its mission in extraordinary circumstances. The most important goal of managing a crisis is to prevent it from destroying the organization's ability to achieve its mission and goals. Whether the mission is charitable, educational or service-oriented, crisis management helps the organization deal with the unthinkable in the present and sustain the nonprofit for the future. The next chapter will review how we define risk management and a practical, five-step risk management process that any nonprofit can use.

Chapter 3
Treatment Methods

P hysicians believe that a consistent approach to identifying and assessing the symptoms results in a more accurate diagnosis and more beneficial course of treatment. Professional risk managers often follow a set method of identifying and managing risk and, we hope, you will come to believe that a systematic approach works for you, as well. Here is a brief review of the definition of risk and the five-step process used by the Nonprofit Risk Management Center.

What Is Risk Management?

While you won't find these definitions in an academic or insurance industry textbook on risk management, we believe that the following phrases aptly define risk and risk management for nonprofit organizations. *Risk* is the possible deviation from what you expect to occur. *Risk management*, therefore, is:

- a discipline for dealing with uncertainty.

- a system for making choices with respect to the clients you serve, the procedures and policies you adopt and the overall way in which you conduct the "business" of your organization.

- a framework for understanding and predicting the potential liability of a nonprofit in the event something goes wrong.

- a strategic approach to identifying exposures, including potential accidents and other losses, before they happen.

- a model for responding to unexpected events and outcomes to minimize the adverse effects of these events.

Risk Management Process Overview

Ideally risk management creates an environment where a nonprofit can take informed risks. The Nonprofit Risk Management Center uses the following five-step Risk Management Process.

Step 1. **Establish the context.**

The risk management process begins with identifying the role of risk within the organization. Some organizations are risk averse while others are extreme risk takers. Where the organization falls on the continuum will affect the context of your risk management program. Another consideration is how important the practice of risk management is to the organization and the level of resources it's willing to commit to the process. Ideally the board and senior management should support and encourage the use of effective risk management techniques. To establish the context for your nonprofit, it's helpful to define the relationships between the organization and its environment (the needs it meets, the legal and regulatory parameters, etc.). Another key step is identifying the organization's overall strengths and weaknesses and the opportunities and threats it faces. Consider the various factors that might support or impair your ability to manage the risks your nonprofit faces.

Risk Management Process

establish the context → acknowledge & identify risk → evaluate and prioritize risk → implement risk management techniques → monitor and update the program

Step 2. **Identify risk.**

Risk identification is essentially the process of determining what can happen, why and how. In most small to mid-size nonprofits, a committee comprising staff and volunteers undertakes this step to identify the nonprofit's risks in a brainstorming session. You can organize the brainstorming around asset categories (people, property, income and reputation) or by the departments or operational units in your organization (such as administration, finance, governance, development/fundraising, conference/events, communications, client services and information technology).

Step 3. **Evaluate and prioritize risk.**

Not every risk facing a nonprofit is likely to materialize. Other risks may be likely but their consequences not especially severe. Here is where we make sense of risk and set priorities by evaluating the likelihood of a risk materializing and its potential severity. For example, while the risk of physical abuse to a client of the organization may be extremely small, the costs — both human and financial — could be devastating if it occurred.

Step 4. **Decide how to control your risks and implement the risk management program using available tools.**

This is the most active phase of the process. The committee develops strategies to minimize the likelihood of a risk materializing and responses that will be activated should an incident occur. The tools in the risk management process are: avoidance, modification, sharing and retention. These strategies are then tested by the organization. Low-priority risks should be accepted and monitored.

Step 5. **Monitor and update the risk management program as needed.**

Risk management is a circular process. Each of the five steps of the process is connected to the steps that precede and follow it. The team assigned to risk management in a nonprofit organization should review the techniques it has implemented on an annual basis to make any revisions that may be needed. Each year the risk management committee can also select a new set of risks on which to focus its attention.

Risk Management Committees

Some of the larger U.S. nonprofits employ full-time, professional risk managers to coordinate such risk management activities as loss control efforts, claims reporting, insurance purchasing, and safety program implementation. Some organizations use an outside advisor to assist in creating a risk management program. But for many nonprofits, budget limitations rule out the use of risk management professionals.

For such organizations, a risk management committee is a highly effective tool for addressing risk management needs. The committee can function either in lieu of a professional risk manager or as a valuable and supportive partner to the agency's risk manager.

The committee is a group of people charged with developing and overseeing an organization's risk management program. The goals and activities of the risk management committee depend entirely on the specific needs of the nonprofit. For example, in some organizations the committee may take the nonprofit through the risk management process described in this chapter. This work may include identifying insurable risks facing the nonprofit and working with an insurance advisor (an agent, broker or consultant) to secure coverage for the nonprofit. In other organizations the committee may be formed to address a particular safety concern, such as the risks of a proposed special event, or changes that the organization seeks to make following an accident or catastrophe.

Now, let's get down to analyzing, preventing and surviving a crisis.

Chapter 4
Treatment Phases

E very nonprofit is at risk of facing a crisis. In fact, we believe that nonprofits should consider not whether, but *when* they might have a crisis on their hands. We can seldom control how or where a crisis will occur. What we can control is how we prepare for, react to and respond in a crisis situation.

In health care you can cure some patients and others you can only treat to alleviate symptoms and improve the individual's quality of life. Managing crisis in a nonprofit is similar: you can avoid some crises thereby "curing" the nonprofit's ills, but some crises are unavoidable; no matter what you do, the treatment can only lessen the symptoms' effects and help the nonprofit function to capacity and survive.

When immersed in a crisis that tests the mettle of senior managers and threatens the survival of a nonprofit, it isn't unusual to feel that suddenly, everything has gone terribly wrong. The crisis may be escalating rapidly. Many in the organization may believe that little could have been done to prevent the crisis and that even less can be done to alter its course. A closer examination of the causes and development of a crisis reveals that a crisis rarely occurs "all of a sudden." There is actually a series of phases in every crisis. A major determinant of how well an organization will cope in the vortex of a crisis is how well it has addressed the phases occurring before the "you know what" hits the fan.

The steps an organization takes months or even years before a crisis occurs may be just as important as its immediate response to the full force of a crisis. Consideration of the pre-event phases will also position a nonprofit to act thoughtfully and strategically in the most vulnerable and chaotic moments of its history.

Phase 1: **Anticipating a Crisis**

Create a Framework for Crisis Planning

Begin by simply setting aside time to discuss crisis planning with several key staff members. Form a working group or crisis management committee with shared responsibility and start developing a plan. Each person should agree to take on specific tasks and set dates for completion in order to move the process along. Schedule regular times to get back together and report on progress, maybe once a month or so. The important thing is to establish regular times when you will focus on crisis preparedness.

In small nonprofits, the crisis management committee will probably have the same makeup as the risk management team. In large nonprofits, the crisis management team could be a subcommittee or a task force of the larger risk management committee. Either way you want key functions of the nonprofit represented.

The committee's role is strategic. For the well-being of your nonprofit, it functions both as a diagnostician and a treatment specialist. The diagnostician is a medical specialist brought into difficult cases, usually affecting multiple body systems, who analyzes the patient's symptoms in totality and determines the cause in order that the disease specialist(s) can prescribe treatment. Similarly, the committee scrutinizes core functions of the nonprofit to identify and, in many cases, reduce or eliminate risks that could throw the organization into crisis mode. As indicated in Chapter 3, the committee might examine operations by looking at categories of assets or by considering operational units or departments such as administration, fundraising and service delivery.

There are several important points to keep in mind as you get started. Remember that you can't totally avoid some risk without ceasing operations and abandoning your mission. Crisis management isn't about curtailing the work of your nonprofit or limiting its positive impact. On the contrary, the intent of crisis management is to enable your organization to minimize the damage from adverse events and resume normal operations as soon as possible.

Keep in mind that just one incident could plunge your entire organization into a crisis. That's all it takes. Thus, it's critical that you develop a crisis management plan, disseminate the plan throughout the organization and work to achieve buy-in from all personnel through consistent review and training.

Inventory Assets

It's important to conduct an inventory of vital assets in the anticipation phase, because it might be impossible to do so in the aftermath or a crisis. What assets? Consider all of the property, both on and off premises, you need and use to achieve your mission. If you returned to your building tomorrow and discovered it was uninhabitable, would you be able to recall the number of telephones, filing cabinets, CPUs and the equipment previously used to deliver services? Assuming you have insurance to cover your losses, a detailed inventory that survives the fire, flood or other disaster will make the process of working with claims adjusters a less painful one. Additional pieces of important information include whether the property is owned or leased, and relevant identifying information, such as brand names, model names or numbers, serial numbers, lessors, leasing agreement numbers — all the details you require for replacement or remuneration.

If your facility includes offices, as well as service delivery equipment (such as recreational or playground equipment, a computer learning center or medical equipment), you might develop separate inventories based on the different uses of your facility. Critical records should also be inventoried. These include insurance forms, leases, partnership agreements, and client, volunteer and funder databases. You will need copies on site for reference and use; backup copies should be kept off site in a lockbox or in your attorney's office. Wherever possible, use existing sources of information to compile your inventory, such as an up-to-date fixed assets schedule.

A sample worksheet for inventorying vital assets is provided on the next page.

Identify Crisis Risks

If the range of crises that might befall a nonprofit is so vast, is it helpful or even possible to define specific crisis categories? The answer is yes. Awareness is the first step to preparedness, and an essential step in the risk management process is risk identification: the process of categorizing and anticipating the types of risks an organization faces.

Examples of a crisis or threat are an incident or event that would potentially:

❑ result in serious injury or death,

❑ result in litigation,

❑ deter donors or otherwise impair fundraising goals,

❑ impair the organization's ability to meet its core operating expenses,

❑ render the organization unable to deliver core services, or

SAMPLE
Inventory of Assets Worksheet

Asset Type: **Computer Equipment**
(CPUs, monitors, file servers, universal power supply units, scanners, printers, storage devices, laptops, LCD projectors, cameras, etc.)

Name	Brand	Model	Serial #	Lessor	Lease #	Location	Purchase Date
CPU	Dell	123	23-45-67	XYZ	456	Room 1	2/1/01
Monitor	Dell	TUV	23-46-67	XYZ	456	Room 1	2/1/01
Keyboard	Dell	PRS	23-47-67	XYZ	456	Room 1	2/1/01
Mouse	Dell	MNO	23-48-67	XYZ	456	Room 1	2/1/01

Asset Type: **Furniture**
(desks, filing cabinets, chairs, computer workstations, etc.)

Name	Brand	Model	Serial #	Lessor	Lease #	Location	Purchase Date
Work station	Colby	EFG-1	42169	XYZ	987	Room 1	2/1/01
Task chair	Flexi	42	A9C6	XYZ	987	Room 1	2/1/01
2-drawer file	Colby	EFG-2	42168	XYZ	987	Room 1	2/1/01

Asset Type: **Office Equipment**
(telephones, photocopier, fax machine, scales, postage meter, etc.)

Name	Brand	Model	Serial #	Lessor	Lease #	Location	Purchase Date
Copier	Rox	Vg912	034-68-A	XYZ	100	Room 4	2/1/01
Label printer	MyName	32	BYG	owned	n/a	Room 4	2/1/01
Telephone	Multiline	4	1A62	owned	n/a	Room 4	2/1/01
Calculator	Cusco	412	QR123	owned	n/a	Room 4	2/1/01

Asset Type: **Other Equipment**
(playground equipment, athletic equipment, medical equipment, etc.)

Name	Brand	Model	Serial #	Lessor	Lease #	Location	Purchase Date

Asset Type: **Databases**
(client, volunteer, funder)

Description	Location	Purchase Date

Asset Type: **Documents**
(leases, partnership agreements, etc.)

Description	Location	Purchase Date

❑ garner negative publicity and media attention, resulting in the death of the organization.

Crisis risks can be categorized in a number of ways. Some experts separate "human-initiated" crises from nature-related crises that occur without human intervention. For the purpose of this discussion, we differentiate crisis risks into the following two categories: avoidable (or preventable) and unavoidable (or unpreventable).

Avoidable Crises Risks

To help you identify the avoidable crises that might befall your nonprofit, consider the following potential causes of a crisis in a nonprofit:

■ **Financial Difficulties.** Thankfully, many nonprofits have yet to experience the types of crises described thus far. However, nearly every nonprofit has at one time experienced financial difficulties. From the challenge of getting an organization under way with only meager resources, to surviving the loss of grant funding or a donor's decision to discontinue support, to facing higher-than-anticipated expenses for a major undertaking, few nonprofits have escaped the challenge or crisis caused by inadequate financial resources. It's an experience that binds nonprofits in an indestructible brotherhood. These war stories are often shared at networking events attended by nonprofit CEOs and other managers. Many nonprofits weather the storm of financial crisis with little fanfare and minimal notice by stakeholders. Monies are borrowed from Peter to pay Paul, and the looming crisis of meeting tomorrow's payroll is averted. In other cases, a generous benefactor rides up to the nonprofit's doorstep on a white horse or a bank reluctantly establishes a line of credit in the nick of time. Sometimes, however, serious financial difficulty takes root and a major crisis is on hand. Some organizations wither under the strain and eventually disappear. Others find a way to survive, vowing to protect the organization more effectively and avoid future crises.

■ **Actual or Alleged Client Maltreatment.** In an organization where criminal conduct is unimaginable, the risk of hurting — instead of helping — clients may be overlooked. Unfortunately, every year, the activities of some nonprofits cause harm to the intended beneficiaries of nonprofit services. In many cases this harm is unintentional and results from lack of training, inadequate facilities or equipment, or just plain accidents. In rare instances, clients are harmed through the reckless or intentional acts of paid or volunteer staff. Almost without exception, just the accusation of client maltreatment will cause a crisis for a nonprofit service provider.

Crisis Management Checklist

- ❑ Isolate the crisis from the organization.

- ❑ Assume control.

- ❑ Assess damages.

- ❑ Account for personnel.

Every organization serving vulnerable clients should have a plan in place that triggers an immediate, compassionate and thorough response to the reporting of client maltreatment. At the same time, the accused should be treated fairly. Remember that accusations can be unprovable or false. Keep in mind that some allegations and certain types of service providers may be subject to mandatory reporting laws. For many nonprofits, no category of crisis is more likely to jeopardize their survival. Any instance of client maltreatment is a potential precursor to negative publicity, public outrage, costly litigation and serious threats to an organization's ability to survive.

- ■ **Service or Product Failure**. Every organization that boasts about its success rate, rehabilitation activities, safety record or other standard of performance is at risk of a crisis stemming from the failure to deliver the product or service as expected or promised. A crisis may result from an organization's inability to meet a service delivery goal or quota established by a government or private sector funder. A crisis may loom when the students at a charter school fail to meet the high academic standards promoted by the organization. Or an organization that relies on the proceeds of an annual fund-raising event to cover its operating expenses may face a crisis when the fire marshal cancels the event.

- ■ **Accidents**. Accidents happen. Accidents occur even in organizations with capable staffs and solid risk management programs. From human miscalculations to equipment failures, the causes of accidents are innumerable. A minor accident is unlikely to cause a crisis. A major accident involving serious injury, death or the destruction of facilities can permanently cripple an organization. Many accidents can be averted. And every accident, large or small, can be handled in a manner that reduces the overall loss or damage sustained by the nonprofit.

- ■ **Transportation-related Mishaps.** Closely-related to the general category of accidents but significant enough to require separate attention is the risk of transportation-related accidents and mishaps. Every nonprofit, including those that don't own any vehicles, is exposed to loss and harm from the transportation of clients, staff members and volunteers in vehicles. Whether it's a two-vehicle accident or an accident involving a bus full of young clients, serious auto accidents are a common cause of crisis in the nonprofit sector.

- ■ **Guilt by Association.** In some respects, a scandal is like a bacteria or virus that has the ability to spread from one unsuspecting victim to the next without great fanfare. Nonprofits exist in an interconnected world. We benefit — and suffer — from the good fortune and scandals faced by sister organizations, affiliates, parent organizations and even associations to which we belong. When a scandal affects one organization in the sector, reverberations are often felt by dozens of others. The early 1990s scandal involving the United Way of America made it more difficult for hundreds of United Way affiliates throughout the nation to raise funds for worthy causes and washed over other organizations, as well. All nonprofits were forced to be more forthcoming about how the funding they raised was being spent. Likewise, the embezzlement by the treasurer of the Episcopal Church in the late 1990s called into question the adequacy of safeguards to prevent theft in religious institutions across the United States.

■ **Employment Dispute.** Many nonprofit managers know that the organization's most vital asset, its employees, can also be the greatest potential threat or risk to the organization's stability, solvency and survival. When an employee tenders a formal allegation of sexual harassment, discrimination, retaliation or other inappropriate action, the nonprofit may be facing a crisis. The powerful and destructive weapons available to an angry staff member are greater today than at any previous time. Dashing off an accusatory missive requires only the computer equipped with e-mail, which was provided to the employee by the nonprofit. In a matter of seconds and with a click of the mouse, your staff member's complaint can be lodged with government regulators, your congressman, the media, and even with current and potential donors.

Lawsuits remain a powerful weapon for disgruntled employees who may feel that an employer owes them. One of the downsides of nonprofits' zeal to take on the strategic practices of well-regarded private businesses is the likelihood that employees will also view the nonprofit as a successful business that should be accountable to its employees. As nonprofits successfully establish large endowment funds, begin investing financial reserves and purchase comprehensive insurance protection, employees are less likely to feel charitable about the organization's status as a charity. Instead of seeing the nonprofit as an organization scrambling to serve clients with meager resources, employees may view the nonprofit as a deep pocket, a view that may not be completely wrong.

■ **Criminal Conduct.** Every nonprofit CEO and board of directors likes to think that the organization attracts good-hearted, honest and trustworthy individuals. No one wants to imagine that predators, thieves or violent criminals are in the applicant pool. But as has been seen from time to time, nonprofits aren't immune to the criminal element. Individuals inclined to commit criminal acts apply for and have been appointed to positions in nonprofits throughout the United States. Unfortunately, there is no single fail-safe test that can be administered to identify — 100 percent of the time — convicted or prospective criminals when they are in your applicant pool. Even a criminal history background check won't reveal the intentions of a would-be or first-time offender or someone who has never been caught.

When a crime is committed against a nonprofit, a crisis may result. The organization may survive the theft of a few office supplies, but the embezzlement of a large sum could devastate the organization, leaving it without the resources needed to deliver vital services. In the latter case, a nonprofit must respond effectively on two fronts: continue to operate despite compromised financial resources; and respond to criticism and scrutiny from the media, as well as disappointed donors, members, volunteers and other key constituents.

One way to identify weaknesses in your internal controls that might needlessly expose you to theft, is to consider how a person might steal from your nonprofit. Is blank check stock easily accessible? Would anyone notice if a check payable to an unknown vendor appeared on the bank statement? And if you believe your controls are pretty effective, how might an insider get around them to access your financial assets?

An expert in the area of child abuse prevention says, "Where there's smoke, there's usually fire" to emphasize the critical need to follow up hunches or other suspicions about an applicant's background or motivations. A common characteristic of individuals who prey on children for sexual gratification is their extreme enthusiasm about working with children and their lack of appropriate adult relationships. Checking additional references and pursuing red flags are keys to identifying people who represent a high risk of harm.

Unavoidable Crisis Risks

■ **Natural Disasters**, such as tornadoes, hurricanes, earthquakes, floods, mudslides and wildfires are unavoidable. These are so-called "acts of God," and you can't reduce the probability of these events occurring. What you can do is identify which ones are inherent to your area of the country, and of those, which ones are more likely to strike your nonprofit. Then you can take steps to make certain that your nonprofit is as prepared as practically and reasonably possible to cope with the events when and if they unfold.

■ **Other** unavoidable risks are bomb threats, arson, utility failure/leaks, Hazmat incidents, terrorist strikes and the sudden deaths of your CEO, board chair, a client or a volunteer. Some of the procedures you put in place will reduce the probability of these incidents occurring or the damage they cause, but they really are out of your control. For instance, a sound personnel policy can reduce the probability that an employee or ex-employee will set fire to your building; however, your building can be targeted for arson just because it's there and someone is determined to see it go up in flames. Nothing you can do.

To move your crisis management committee along, divide and conquer the types of crises and determine which ones are most likely to affect your nonprofit. One approach is to focus on the most likely crisis risks first, mindful of your resource constraints. Another approach is to tackle the avoidable crisis risks, such as discrimination, first and the unavoidable crisis risks, such as natural disasters, second. By analyzing the avoidable crises first, the crisis management committee may significantly reduce or mitigate them so they pose much less of a threat to the well-being of your nonprofit's mission. The crisis assessment will help you make these determinations.

Conduct a Crisis Assessment

Like its risk management cousin — the risk assessment — a *crisis assessment* is a thoughtful assessment of vulnerabilities. However, instead of focusing broadly on any risk facing the organization that could impede its ability to achieve its mission, a crisis assessment shines the spotlight on risks that would throw the organization into crisis mode. Some people refer to this process as a threat assessment.

One way to conduct a crisis assessment is to use the worksheets that follow and determine whether each category applies to your nonprofit. Start with the avoidable crises, such as harassment, and then tackle the unavoidable crises, such as a Hazmat incident. (If you have enough people involved in the process, you might split the crisis management committee in two and assign one half to the avoidable crisis assessment and the other half to the unavoidable crisis assessment.) Continue by assigning frequency and severity ratings to each identified threat. A frequency rating estimates how often this crisis might materialize, if at all. You can rate these 5=high, 3=moderate or 1=low. A severity rating is based on your assessment of how bad the crisis would be if it does occur. Put another way, a severity rating measures how costly it would be to fix the situation and restore operations. Indicate a numeric score in the space next to each identified crisis: 5=highly likely or very costly, 3=not likely or moderate cost, and 1=highly unlikely or inexpensive. Add the two numbers to determine an overall score.

Avoidable Crisis Assessment (Level 1) Worksheet

SAMPLE

Check off the types of crisis that you might expect to afflict your nonprofit.

Type	Could It Happen Here? Yes	No	If yes, how likely? (5=very likely 3=it could 1=not likely)	How bad would it be? (5=very bad, significant cost; 3=bad, moderate cost; 1=not so bad, inexpensive)
Financial difficulties				
Funding source dries up				
Consolidation or merger	X		3	3
Loses interest in the cause		X		
Goes bankrupt		X		
Cash flow uneven	X		5	3
Event/campaign proceeds less than anticipated	X		3	5
Client Maltreatment				
Sexual abuse				
By staff or volunteer	X		1	5
By another client		X		
Physical abuse				
By staff or volunteer	X		1	5
By another client		X		
Service or Product Failure				
Food Poisoning (food bank, special event)		X		
Other: Web site hacked	X		3	5
Accidents				
Slip, trip and fall by client or general public	X		3	1
Fire	X		3	3
Household-chemical spill		X		
Guilt by Association				
Major scandal affects				
One of our "partners"	X		1	3
Our segment of the nonprofit "world," e.g. United Way	X		1	5
Workplace violence				
By employee	X		1	3
By employee's significant other	X		1	5
Employment dispute				
Allegation of discrimination	X		2	3
Allegation of harassment	X		1	3
Other:				
Criminal Conduct				
Theft by staff or volunteer	X		1	1
Property/equipment theft	X		1	2

Unavoidable Crisis Assessment (Level 2) Worksheet

Organization: <u>ABC Nonprofit</u>

Unavoidable Risks	Applicable?	Frequency	Severity/Cost	TOTAL SCORE
Natural disasters				
Hurricane	☐ yes ■ no			
Tornado	☐ yes ■ no			
Windstorm	■ yes ☐ no	3	2	5
Hailstorm	■ yes ☐ no	3	3	6
Earthquake	☐ yes ■ no			
Landslide (mudslide)	☐ yes ■ no			
Flood	☐ yes ■ no			
Fire (wildfire)	☐ yes ■ no			
Other incidents				
Bomb threat	☐ yes ■ no			
Fire	■ yes ☐ no	1	3	4
Utility failure/leak	■ yes ☐ no	3	3	6
Hazmat incident	☐ yes ■ no			
Sudden death				
CEO	■ yes ☐ no	1	4	5
Board Chair	■ yes ☐ no	1	3	4
Client	■ yes ☐ no	3	5	8
Volunteer	■ yes ☐ no	1	5	6
Computer hacked	■ yes ☐ no	3	2	5
Significant equipment-theft or data loss	☐ yes ■ no			
Hostage threat	☐ yes ■ no			
Terrorism	■ yes ☐ no	1	8	9
Workplace violence	■ yes ☐ no	1	5	6
Other				
_____	☐ yes ☐ no			
_____	☐ yes ☐ no			
_____	☐ yes ☐ no			

Develop a Risk Financing Strategy

Your nonprofit's risk financing strategy should answer the question, "How will we pay for harm caused by our operations or for losses stemming from a crisis?" A financing strategy for insurable risks (such as the risk that property will be stolen or an employment-related suit will be filed) is essential to avoiding a crisis caused by lack of financial resources. Simply deciding in advance how you will pay for harm caused by intentional or unintentional acts can stop a crisis in its tracks or stop an event from spiraling into a crisis. For example, if someone suffers a minor injury while on your premises, does your organization have resources (savings, insurance or a line of credit) to pay for the victim's medical expenses? If your nonprofit is sued, do you have pro bono counsel on call or have you purchased a liability policy that requires the insurer to defend your nonprofit?

There are various potential sources of funds to pay for losses. Commercial insurance is a common source of financing, but it isn't the only option available to a nonprofit, nor is it appropriate (or even available) for every type of loss. While every nonprofit is vulnerable to a crisis, many organizations can't afford to purchase even a relatively inexpensive insurance policy. Remember, too, that not every risk can be insured; insurance can never compensate a nonprofit for damage to its reputation in a community.

The following is a suggested approach to getting started:

Step 1. ***Identify and engage an insurance advisor for your nonprofit*** — An insurance advisor is one of several outside professionals few nonprofits can do without. A suitable advisor is an insurance agent, broker or risk management consultant who understands nonprofits and is willing to take the time to get to know your organization and the climate in which you do business.

Step 2. ***Identify the sources and potential crises facing your nonprofit*** — Discuss the critical areas of concern on your *Avoidable Crisis Assessment Worksheet* and the *Unavoidable Crisis Assessment Worksheet* with your insurance advisor (see the blank forms on pages 73 and 74). You might want to tackle the avoidable crisis risks first or split the avoidable and unavoidable between two halves of your crisis management committee.

Step 3. ***Identify applicable coverages and potential gaps*** — Work with your insurance advisor to review the list of crises identified during your brainstorming exercise and determine which, if any, insurance products could be helpful in the event the crisis materializes.

Step 4. ***Establish new goals for your risk-financing program*** — Identify options for strengthening your insurance program or other risk-financing measures with the goal of making certain that financial resources are accessible that will enable your nonprofit to survive a crisis.

Acknowledge Financial Vulnerabilities and Take Action

One common source of nonprofit sector crisis is poor financial health. Few nonprofits have escaped the occasional or persistent aches and stresses of financial difficulty. A nonprofit's history contains a lot of information needed to avoid this form of generally preventable crisis. Consider constructing a financial "HistoryGram" following the steps below:

Step 1. *Play Financial Diagnostician* — Identify the financial low-points in your nonprofit's history.

Step 2. *Identify Key Stressors* — Indicate the key characteristics of each low-point (e.g., inadequate cash or unexpected expense).

Step 3. *Identify Causes* — Note the precipitating events or causes (e.g., donor withdrew support or annual fundraiser generated less than expected).

Step 4. *Map Warning Signs* — Describe the warning signs that, with hindsight, were visible months or more before the low-points.

Step 5. *Note Preventive Measures* — Describe what was done (if anything) to avoid the situation or prevent it from spiraling.

Step 6. *Develop an Action Plan* — Describe what could have been done to avoid the situation or minimize its negative effects.

Step 7. *Conduct a Recurrence Assessment* — Indicate whether the causes described in Step 3 and outcome identified in Step 1 could recur.

Step 8. *Develop a Strategy* — Describe your plan to avoid the risks or cope more effectively if the low-point occurs again.

A sample worksheet appears on the next page. It suggests one approach to completing a Financial Crisis HistoryGram for your nonprofit.

Forewarned is forearmed. Nothing can better help you in dealing with crisis than being prepared for one before it occurs. Even a minimal amount of preparation can prevent many minor crises from ever occurring and can help keep potentially major crises in the minor leagues.

Financial Crisis HistoryGram

Describe past financial crisis	Could it happen again?	Could we have prevented it?	How?	Have we done this? If not, have we set a target date?
Emergency shelter grant was not renewed, forcing us to close shelter with only 30 days notice.	■ Yes ❑ No	■ Yes ❑ No	Avoid reliance on single funding source for mission-critical activity. That way, the non-renewal of funding by one source would only require scaling back operations.	❑ Yes ■ No 3 months
Donation check bounced in July 2001.	■ Yes ❑ No	❑ Yes ■ No		■ Yes ❑ No Donor went bankrupt. In the future, we will not write checks against large donations until these donations clear our account.
Series of checks to key vendors bounces in October 2001.	❑ Yes ■ No	■ Yes ❑ No	Make journal entries daily instead of monthly, so that funds can be trans-ferred from savings to checking account in time to meet current expenses.	■ Yes ❑ No New controller hired and accounts are kept up to date.
Donations were down by 40% during last quarter of 2000.	■ Yes ❑ No	■ Yes ❑ No	Keeping closer tabs on receipts will enable us to respond with a special solicitation or take other steps to compensate for poor fundraising results.	■ Yes ❑ No

Consider Contingencies

A contingency plan is nothing more than a document that details carefully considered alternative courses of action. These alternatives can be "activated" or selected when a crisis renders a nonprofit's principal delivery/operational strategy ineffective or impossible. For example, an organization that holds its annual fund-raiser outdoors should have a contingency plan in the event inclement weather makes it unsafe or unrealistic to hold the event as planned. Several contingencies may be identified, including:

❑ postponing the event,

❑ setting up tents on the morning of the fund-raiser in the event rain is forecast,

❑ holding the event at an alternative, indoor location, such as a gymnasium, or

❑ purchasing "weather insurance" to cover the organization's losses should indoor alternatives be unacceptable and canceling the event is necessary.

The contingency options should be carefully evaluated and an organization should have an idea of its likely choice of alternatives. If possible, the list should be put in order — with the most likely, feasible option listed first. A Sample Contingency Planning Worksheet appears below.

Contingency Planning Worksheet

Event or activity: Annual Fundraiser to be held outdoors

Possible Snags	Options	What needs to be done?	By whom?
1. Weather	Set up tents.	Check tent rental prices.	Mary
	Use indoor location.	ID alternative location.	Joe
	Purchase bad weather insurance.	Obtain a quote.	Rick
	Postpone.	Discuss with board.	Sarah
2. Ticket sales less than budgeted	Reduce expenses. Solicit another sponsor. Cancel/postpone event.		

Call Someone Who Cares

Does your organization have the relationships it'll need to survive a crisis? If you've completed *Avoidable Crisis Worksheet* on page 26 and *Unavoidable Crisis Worksheet* on page 27, review your list of crisis risks with this question in mind.

Few nonprofits have the resources necessary to survive a crisis without outside help. From moral support to emergency cash to medical assistance, organizations in crisis are highly dependent on others. While you can hope that a variety of organizations will come forward to help in your time of need, it's far better to establish and maintain solid relationships with the organizations you can imagine needing in a crisis. For example, if your facilities are temporarily unavailable due to fire, flood or a criminal investigation, perhaps another nearby service provider could assist your clients on an interim basis. Two organizations providing similar services in a community might work out an arrangement whereby each calls on the other in the event a crisis makes it impossible for one to meet client needs.

The following sample worksheet is provided to help you begin to consider, record and take action with respect to forming or strengthening key relationships.

SAMPLE

Crisis Management Relationships Worksheet

List the needs your organization would having during a crisis. Identify the potential sources of help, and how the source could provide other assistance that would strengthen your ability to survive a crisis.

What do we need?	Who can provide?	Do we have an arrangement?	How does it help?	How else could it help?
Cots	American Red Cross	■ yes □ no	provides cots	help identify other emergency shelter providers
Medical supplies	American Red Cross	■ yes □ no	provides supplies	help identify other sources for supplies and equipment
Water and food for clients	ABC Co.	■ yes □ no	provide food and water	help with on-site distribution

Communicate to Constituencies

Many nonprofits facing a crisis need to communicate a message quickly and to a diverse audience. For instance, a school administrator needs to communicate with emergency medical personnel and police, parents of children attending the school, families of teachers and other staff, professionals who can provide crisis counseling and other support, local and national media, and possibly others following an incident of violence. Before the crisis looms is the time to consider the following:

- ❑ Who will we/might we need to contact in the event of a crisis? Consider all of the constituencies served by the organization, as well as groups affected by the nonprofit's operations, or to whom the nonprofit must be accountable.

- ❑ How will we get in touch? What will be the best way to make contact: telephone tree, e-mail, broadcast fax, a news conference, pagers, wireless phones, public address system, intercom?

- ❑ What backup system is available if our primary means of communication is compromised?

- ❑ Is the list of personnel we would/might need to contact readily available to more than one staff member?

- ❑ Will one person make all of the phone calls, or will a group of people be mobilized to reach constituents as quickly as possible?

Constituent Contact Worksheet

A current list of constituent contacts is important to the lifeblood of your nonprofit. Rank them in order of importance. List ways to reach them. Assign who will reach them in a crisis. Keep copies of the list at home, at work and in your Crisis Management Manual.

Rank	People	Organization	Best Method	By Whom?
1	CEO	ABC Nonprofit	wireless phone (000) 555-3333	Crisis Team Captain
2	Board chair	ABC Nonprofit	wireless phone (000) 555-6666	Crisis Team Captain
3	Department Heads	ABC Nonprofit	list follows	CEO
4	Staff	ABC Nonprofit	list follows	Department heads
5	Clients	ABC Nonprofit	list follows	Assigned staff who know them
6	Vendors	Various	telephone	Crisis Team Captain
7	Funders	Various	telephone	CEO

❑ Has everyone who will be contacting constituents received some training in crisis communications? Will everyone the nonprofit will be relying on know what to say, how to deliver critical information effectively and to mitigate risk?

Plan to Act

An organization's "action plan" answers the critical question: "What will we do if a crisis occurs?" In some cases, aspects of your response may remain the same, despite the cause — or source — of the crisis. For example, an important step in your action plan may be conducting a quick review of your insurance coverage and filing claims with your insurers, as appropriate. Or making a call to your insurance advisor (agent, broker or consultant) to keep him or her apprised of the situation and to solicit support and assistance. In other instances, specific types of crises may require unique responses. Following the sudden death of the CEO, most nonprofit board presidents would quickly convene the board of directors — either by telephone or in person. But bringing the board together for a face-to-face meeting may be "overkill" after a former employee sues the organization for wrongful termination. One strategy for formulating an action plan is to revisit the major crisis risks identified in the two *Avoidable Crisis Assessment Worksheet* and *Unavoidable Crisis Assessment Worksheet* (on pages 26 and 27) and document possible action steps on a worksheet similar to the sample below.

Crisis Action Overview Worksheet

Crisis Risk	Total Score	Is This Risk Avoidable?	What should be done to keep this risk from happening?	If this risk happens, what should be done immediately?	Resources we need, but not available at present time
cash flow uneven	8	■ Yes ❑ No	Monitor exp. and income weekly and adjust spending	Delay purchases, reduce expenses. Identify ways to reduce cost of ongoing projects.	Bookkeeper
Web site hacked	6	■ Yes ❑ No	Add firewall, change passwords every 60-90 days. Identify tech support providers	Call emergency tech support.	Tech support on call, 24/7

Crisis Action Steps Worksheet

A.   Brainstorm: What are all the steps needed to get from A to Z?

(Guides for Brainstorming
We brainstorm to get out all possible ideas.
1.   mention all ideas; the more ideas, the better.
2.   repetition is okay; people are thinking about their ideas and may miss hearing an idea mentioned, thus they repeat it.
3.   no discussion; no face-making, hisses, sighs, cheers, no judging of anyone's ideas.

Appoint a recorder to write down all ideas large enough for everyone to see.)

B. Rank steps in order of priority #1, #2, #3.

(Break into groups of three to five people. Ask each group to decide the sequence of events necessary to accomplish the task. Have each group report back their conclusions. Have the recorder keep a second list showing the relationships the members find.)

C. List steps and notes.

(When sequence of steps varies, discuss and reach agreement. Recorder can note rationale for sequence next to the step – helpful when making adjustments later.)

D. Create a flowchart: visualize action.

(Put each step in a box and position boxes to show that step's relationship to subsequent and previous steps. For instance, if the step is to douse the fire with water and that action quenches the fire, that's the end. However, if water doesn't put out the fire, the next step would be to pull the fire alarm, and then get the people safely out of the building.)

E. Prepare safety checklist.

(Pull together a list of tips that people need to have as "ready reference" in this emergency.)

Put Together a Crisis Management Manual

When all around you people are losing their heads, you want to hold on to yours. One simple way to help everyone on the team focus in an emergency is with a Crisis Management Manual. The manual functions as a checklist of what to do when and whom to call when. Each nonprofit's manual reflects the most likely scenarios it will have to face and suggests a method for handling those crises. Using the checklists and worksheets throughout this book, you'll be able to create this reference guide for your nonprofit. We suggest you keep the format simple and easy to read; use plenty of short sentences and bulleted phrases. Use charts to show the flow of responsibilities and actions. This gives a visual quick-reference of what the individual should do. Actually include boxes that can be checked when completed. Major divisions could be Avoidable Crises, Unavoidable Crisis, Media, Appendix. Each tab should indicate the crisis for easy access. A sample table of contents and Response Flowchart to use as a springboard to developing your own manual follow:

Table of Contents
Crisis Management Manual

Introduction
    Crisis Management
    Crisis Response Team Members
    Crisis Management Committee Members
    Types of Crises ABC Nonprofit Faces

Avoidable Crises
    Computer Network Impairment
        Computer Network Response Plan
        Computer Network Response
    Fire
        Fire Response Plan
        Fire Response
    Theft
        Theft Response Plan
        Theft Response

Unavoidable Crises
    Arson
        Fire Response Plan
        Fire Response
    Illness/Death
        Illness/Death Response Plan
        Illness/Death Response
    Natural Disaster *(Flood, High Wind, Mudslide)*
        Natural Disaster Response Plan
        Natural Disaster Response
    Utility Failure *(Power, Water Main, Natural Gas)*
        Utility Failure Response Plan
        Utility Failure Response

Fire Response Plan

Actions to take:
- A. When alarm sounds, everyone leaves the building.
  - Use stairways unless smoke-filled. Don't use elevators or escalators.
  - Close doors and windows as you leave. Don't lock.
  - Move beyond the sidewalk or cross the street at the light and gather in front of EFG building for personal safety.
- B. When the alarm is false; it stops, which tells everyone to re-enter the building. If the alarm continues to ring, everyone remains outside the building and waits for the fire trucks to arrive.
- C. If there is a fire and the fire department hasn't arrived, call the fire department and report the location of the fire. Everyone remains outside the building.
- D. (Only use a fire extinguisher if you're trained to use it and the fire is small. Do this only after fire alarm is ringing.)
- E. Fire department personnel decide how to manage utilities.
- F. Fire department gives OK before anyone re-enters the building.

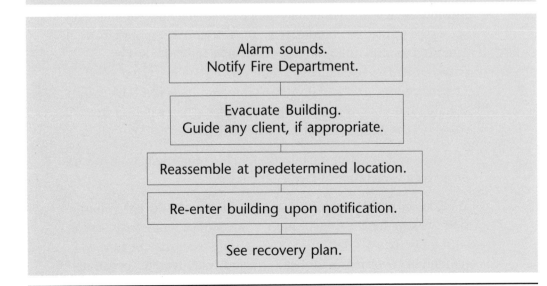

Alarm sounds.
Notify Fire Department.

Evacuate Building.
Guide any client, if appropriate.

Reassemble at predetermined location.

Re-enter building upon notification.

See recovery plan.

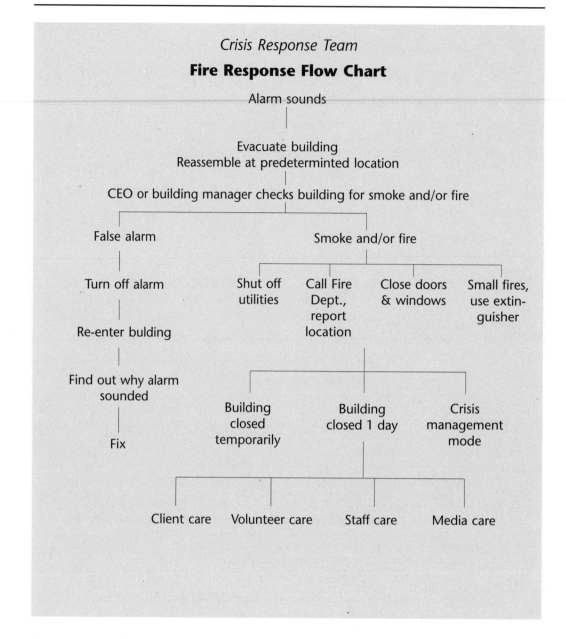

Crisis Response Team
Fire Response Flow Chart

Alarm sounds

Evacuate building
Reassemble at predeterminted location

CEO or building manager checks building for smoke and/or fire

False alarm

Smoke and/or fire

Turn off alarm

Shut off utilities

Call Fire Dept., report location

Close doors & windows

Small fires, use extinguisher

Re-enter buulding

Find out why alarm sounded

Building closed temporarily

Building closed 1 day

Crisis management mode

Fix

Client care

Volunteer care

Staff care

Media care

Form a Crisis Response Team

Authors of various crisis management texts agree that a small team should be formed to coordinate an organization's response to a crisis. The need to form and train the team *before* the crisis hits is paramount. This will be your action team. They will have internalized the drill and be able to think on their feet. They can remain calm under fire and have a presence. They will lead the troops so the nonprofit will survive the crisis.

The composition of an organization's crisis response team will vary based on a wide range of factors, including:

❑ The *size of the organization* — The number of paid and volunteer staff working for the organization. For example, in an organization with more than 50 staff, the crisis response team may include a handful of key department heads (include maintenance personnel or other structural advisors) plus the CEO. In an organization with fewer than 10 paid staff, the crisis response team may include two board members, two staff and two outside professional advisors.

❑ The *nature of the services provided by the organization* — Every nonprofit should consider its operations and circumstances before naming the members of the crisis response team. The composition of a crisis response team at an environmental advocacy group will differ from the team created to respond to a crisis at a daycare center. In the former, the team may include an experienced lobbyist and an environmental scientist. In the latter, the team may include the organization's retained counsel, an expert on child abuse prevention or playground safety, and parents of enrolled children.

❑ The *likely sources/causes of crisis in the organization* — Before forming your team, identify the most likely causes of a crisis in your nonprofit. The two *Crisis Assessment Worksheets* (on pages 26 and 27) are helpful in ranking crisis risks. Is the organization more likely to face a crisis stemming from allegations of client mistreatment or a crisis caused by inadequate financial resources? The ranking of crisis risks will suggest areas of expertise and training that may be required during a crisis and individuals with special talents or expertise may be identified as necessary members of the crisis response team.

❑ The *organization's prior experience responding to a crisis* — One certainty in any crisis situation is that when it's all over, one or more key lessons will have been learned. The type of people whose service will be required or highly valued may be among the lessons learned. An organization reflecting on how it handled a lawsuit may conclude that the nonprofit's insurance advisor would have been a valuable member of the crisis response team. The survivors of a crisis may acknowledge that emergency procedures or equipment are of little use when they haven't been tested.

Decide Who Will Serve

Given the tremendous diversity in the nonprofit sector, it's difficult, if not impossible, to suggest the ideal composition of a crisis response team. However, it's a worthwhile exercise to consider the following individuals or personality types as potential members of your team:

■ **The Top Dog** — Why include the nonprofit's executive director or president in responding to a crisis? There may be several reasons, including:

❑ the executive director can quickly command the respect and attention of key staff and volunteers — he or she is a leader already known to the organization's constituents;

Evacuation Checklist

❑ Shut down computer.

❑ Turn off lights.

❑ Close windows.

❑ Assist clients and other staff as needed.

❑ Close doors behind you as you leave (do NOT lock).

❑ Follow escape route.

❑ Meet at predetermined assembly point.

❑ Make certain everyone is accounted for.

- ❑ the executive director is already empowered to act on behalf of the organization, thus no time-delaying special action is required to grant the CEO the authority needed during a crisis;

- ❑ the executive director may have a broad view of the organization's key constituencies, have strong relationships with key partners and be an effective team builder; and

- ❑ the executive director may be the organization's most effective spokesperson.

If the executive director is on the team, it's natural that he or she also serves as the team leader. If this isn't your choice, the executive director should appoint a leader who will be able to make decisions and build consensus. The executive director may have a leader in mind when he or she appoints the committee, perhaps a senior manager with tenure at the nonprofit or someone with past experience providing leadership in a crisis.

■ **The Devil's Advocate or Resident Cynic** — This individual has no difficulty identifying the potential risks in a fund-raising scheme every other person in the nonprofit regards as genius.

■ **The Mouthpiece** — Every nonprofit should have a predetermined spokesperson in order to be truly prepared for a crisis. Sometimes the best spokesperson is the executive director or CEO. For example, following the airplane crash in the Florida Everglades, Value Jet CEO Lewis Jordan was a highly visible spokesperson for the company, convening press conferences in the days following the crash. At every opportunity and before each update on the crash investigation, Jordan reaffirmed the company's sadness and sympathy for the victims of the crash and the family members of victims. Others adhere to a policy of allowing the CEO to present good news and another spokesperson (a public relations professional or other senior manager) to present bad news. Having a trained backup spokesperson who can fill in if the CEO is otherwise engaged or is integrally involved in the crisis, makes good sense.

■ **The Legal Eagle** — Being able to provide a skillful analysis of potential liability and actions needed to prevent a crisis from turning into a field day for the plaintiff's attorney are lead traits for this member of your team. This master networker is the voice of caution, aware of what he or she doesn't know, who tends a wide network of attorney colleagues who could be tapped if needed. The attorney currently serving on your board may — or may not — be the legal eagle you need for the team.

■ **The Bean Counter** — Every crisis response team should include someone with financial training — the financial whiz whose fingers fly on the keys of an adding machine. This key team member will be able to calculate what different strategies will cost, and keep the team informed about the total bill for crisis response activities.

■ **The Juggler** — The juggler on the crisis response team acts as a project manager. This individual should be someone who is intimately familiar with the organization's programs and services, as well as the talents of other team members. The person should be

Relationship Between the Crisis Management Committee and the Crisis Response Team

Crisis Management Committee

Create crisis management committee.
- ❑ Inventory assets.
- ❑ Determine relationships/partnerships.
- ❑ List constituents.

Analyze risks.
- ❑ Assess preventable crises.
- ❑ Assess unpreventable crises.

Develop prevention plans and put into use.
- ❑ Take steps to prevent crises risks.
- ❑ Outline steps for surviving crises.
- ❑ *Create crisis response team.*
- ❑ Create crisis management manual.

Train people, and evaluate and revise plans on regular basis.
- ❑ Communicate changes.
- ❑ Run and record drills.

Develop building recovery plan.

Crisis Response Team

Develop and oversee implementation of crisis response plan.

Evaluate and revise response plans.
- ❑ Minimally, once a year
- ❑ After each crisis response

Communicate with media and various constituencies.
Identify need for crisis counseling.
- ❑ Wrap up events and status of nonprofit.
- ❑ Call in a professional.

Evaluate response to each incident.
Prepare chronological file of how crisis was handled.
- ❑ Potential legal defense
- ❑ Insurance claims

someone who can remind, cajole, organize and motivate others to keep moving, keep on time and keep in line. Designating a project manager role for the crisis response team takes some of the pressure off the executive director, who must be principally concerned with managing the organization's communications and relationships with key constituents.

■ **The Super** — Every crisis response team should include the person who knows the building inside and out who can help responding professionals such as firefighters, police officers, and emergency medical technicians do their jobs efficiently.

Don't Try to Fit Everyone in Your Pace Car

While it's important to include key personnel on your crisis response team, it's also important to make sure to exclude some individuals who can keep the organization focused on its mission. Remember that when the crisis response team is off planning, someone has to be left behind to deliver services. In addition, while it's important to get "buy in" from every level of the organization, groups that are too large tend to become unwieldy and have difficulty achieving consensus.

Another option is to create one team (primary) to develop the background philosophy and then involve additional staff in creating individual plans. The work is spread out and the primary group becomes responsible for review — more than creation. This approach also helps teach a broader spectrum of staff what goes into a plan and what is generally expected of them during a crisis.

Know How to Reach Them

You assembled a team of people with varying skills and talents. You identified the skills you might need in a crisis and named a group of people to one or more crisis response teams. You gave team members their marching orders, and perhaps practiced a few drills. Now a crisis is at hand and you need to reach them.

A crisis may strike during regular business hours with team members on site and available to move. But you should be prepared to reach your team when a crisis occurs during a holiday, weekend or in the middle of the night. Have a list in the Crisis Management Manual at your desk, at home and on your person and a strategy for reaching team members — wherever they may be. The list should generally contain several numbers for each team member, including office, home, wireless, beeper — whichever numbers of whichever methods they respond to most.

Practice to Prepare

While some responses to a crisis can't be easily rehearsed, others can be simulated, practiced or simply discussed to enhance readiness for the real thing and identify any flaws in the action plan. If your nonprofit provides services to vulnerable clients, including emergency or temporary housing, your evacuation drills should require client participation. Each time the organization conducts a drill, key personnel involved should do a brief self-analysis of the exercise. A written record of the analysis should be maintained by the organization. In between full-blown drills, tabletop exercises keep the strategies and process fresh in the minds of all staff and clients. On rare occasions the value of a drill is realized even before the ink has time to dry on the written analysis of the exercise. In August 1989, an emergency team whose members included 1,000 federal and state employees tested their earthquake response plan in San Francisco. When the Loma Prieta earthquake struck the city just six weeks later, the emergency response team received high marks for its effective handling of medical emergencies and skillful evacuation of affected areas of the city.

Keep a Record of Emergency Drills

Consider using a worksheet like the one featured below to make a record of your emergency drills and note observations about these exercises.

Record of Emergency Drills

Organization: *Anytown Recreation Center*

Nature of Drill: <u>Evacuation of recreation center, 1234 Acme St., Anytown, State</u>

Date/ Time	Participants	Observations	Follow-up status
12/1/01 3:00 pm	Coaches, participants and building staff	Maintenance and cleaning staff seemed unfamiliar with the drill. Some coaches expressed frustration over the disruption in the recreation schedule. The kids were very cooperative.	Meet with cleaning and maintenance team before 1/1/02 to discuss evacuation drills - purpose and procedures. Draft memo outlining the importance of drills, the required participation and support of coaching staff.

Phase 2: **Preventing a Crisis**

Think of the following actions as wellness steps for your organization. The reward will be better programs, fewer claims, fewer crises to handle and improved financial health.

Build an Organization Committed to Safety

"But we've never had an incident!" Too many organizations use a "perfect" safety record as the reason for paying scant attention to safety. Other common "excuses" include:

- We can't afford safety equipment/training/precautions.

- The services we're offering aren't really risky or dangerous.

- We don't have time to do all of the planning involved.

- Our staff is very careful.

The best time to plan your response to a crisis is before it occurs, yet few nonprofit managers have a lot of spare time in which to pursue a special project like crisis planning. Lack of time combined with an "It could never happen here" attitude means an important and necessary task often falls to the bottom of the priority list. Yet few things that you can do after-the-fact, will be as effective as a plan put into place beforehand.

There is an additional excuse that managers use for not getting started with crisis planning. They reason that there are so many different things that might go wrong, that it's almost impossible to prepare for the right thing. This way of thinking is, in a sense, correct. Chances are that the crisis you prepare for won't happen, or, at least, it won't happen exactly as you imagined. This shouldn't deter you. The point of crisis preparedness is to build a practice — a way of thinking — about crisis situations that will allow staff to respond with more skill and confidence than if they had never thought about these issues before. If you've been using the worksheets in this book, you've already narrowed down the universe of crisis risks to a list of the ones most likely to affect your nonprofit.

Yes, planning takes time. Yes, safety improvements can cost money (though often not as much as you would think). Yes, your good fortune could continue to hold. But the question to ask yourself, in the words of the immortal Clint Eastwood, is "Do you feel lucky?" Even if you must invest a few dollars and an hour or two of your time per month, preventing a crisis is far less expensive and traumatic than trying to navigate and survive a crisis. While it's important to have good intentions, we all know where the road paved with them could end. In order to make a difference, your good intentions must be translated into action. The following steps can make your vision of a safer organization a reality.

Step 1. ***Articulate and broadcast your emphatic commitment to safety***. If not already part of your mission statement, make your commitment to safety prominent and unswerving. And send the message to everyone. A growing number of nonprofits are incorporating the word "safe" or "safety" into their mission statements. Others post a safety statement in prominent locations, such as on the wall near the swimming pool, on the side of the organization's van, in a frame on the reception desk in the lobby, on the application for volunteer or paid employment, and/or in the volunteer and employee handbooks.

Step 2. ***Provide the training, equipment and resources needed to deliver services safely.*** Every organization must factor its resources and resource constraints into the decisions about which services it will offer and which safety measures it will use. Nonprofits are extraordinarily creative organizations, and most will explore almost any avenue to get the resources needed to deliver core services. Managers are accustomed to persuading others to respond "yes," from local restaurants that donate food to a shelter to local businesses that employ ex-offender job-program trainees. The commitment to obtaining training and safety equipment and materials deserves equal fervor.

Here are some questions to ask when developing your menu of necessary safety resources:

❑ What resources are needed to deliver our services safely?

❑ What training do our paid and volunteer staff members need to perform their assignments?

❑ What training do our paid and volunteer staff members need to be able to cope with unexpected events?

❑ How can we provide the training needed by our staff at an affordable cost?

❑ Are there local businesses or educational institutions that might be willing to train our staff at little or no cost?

❑ What safety equipment is needed for service delivery activities?

❑ Can we acquire the equipment at a reasonable cost or through a charitable donation at no cost?

Step 3. ***Reward, recognize and celebrate results***. An organization's ability to deliver services safely should be celebrated. Individuals who have demonstrated an exemplary commitment to safety should be singled out for special recognition. Recognition sends a message that safety is important and will be rewarded. When a nonprofit embraces safety as central to its mission, it has incorporated wellness as essential to a healthy future.

Take the High Road With Your Employment Practices

One of the most effective strategies for avoiding a crisis that stems from employee discontent is to "take the high road" in your employment practices. Many nonprofit managers and executives get caught up in adopting sound business practices and forget or neglect to focus on fairness as an important ideal in dealing with employees. Fairness, honesty and compassion are among the most powerful repellants to employment practices complaints and lawsuits. Treating people fairly, applying rules and policies consistently, providing honest feedback about performance, and showing compassion should be the cornerstones of your commitment to your workforce.

When you act in a manner that suggests favoritism, sugarcoat or ignore the poor performance of an employee, act without warning in dismissing staff, or behave callously to employees with medical, attendance or performance issues, you're helping to lower morale and inviting formal complaints. Except in very large nonprofits, the filing of a suit against an organization nearly always marks the beginning of a crisis. Few nonprofits have reserve resources available to devote to the defense of a lawsuit. In every case, time and funds that must be diverted to defend against the allegations or pay a judgment or a settlement, means fewer resources for the nonprofit's community-serving mission.

For a comprehensive look at effective employment practices, see *Taking the High Road: A Guide to Effective and Legal Employment Practices for Nonprofits*, available from the Nonprofit Risk Management Center (www.nonprofitrisk.org).

Make Your Expectations Clear and Provide Explicit Direction

Susan O'Malley, president of the Washington Wizards basketball team, tells a story of an enthusiastic young summer intern. Things went well until the first game of the season. As the game got under way, she spied the young man in the stands cheering wildly — for the opposing team. The next day she called him into her office and asked him to explain his behavior. The young man was completely bewildered by her chagrin. "But," he said with dismay, "you never told me that I had to root for the Wizards!"

The lesson, O'Malley says, is clear: Be explicit about expected behaviors. Even when it seems that certain things are obviously against the rules, such as using the organization's computers to access pornographic or other inappropriate Web sites, or engaging in a sexual relationship with a client, spell out the do's and don'ts. Many crises in the nonprofit sector are caused by human misbehaviors. And many of these potentially devastating crises can be avoided by making your expectations crystal clear.

When you tell all of your staff and volunteers what you expect and require and are explicit in stating prohibitive behaviors and their consequences, you will:

❑ reduce the chance you'll hear, "But I didn't know we weren't allowed to do/say that."

❑ increase the likelihood that key personnel will share your vision of the organization's rules and procedures.

❑ establish the basis for a defense of your actions — demonstrating that policies were in place, communicated and monitored is necessary to mounting a successful defense if your nonprofit faces a legal challenge.

The following worksheet is provided as an example of how you might inventory key behavioral issues in your nonprofit and identify any weaknesses that exist in your current practice of providing clear instructions about what is allowed and prohibited in your environment.

Staff Instructions Worksheet

To identify where weaknesses lie, develop a worksheet listing required staff behaviors at your nonprofit. Use the worksheet to evaluate whether adequate instruction has been provided and determine what additional follow-up is needed.

Required Behaviors	Adequate instruction provided to:		Additional follow-up required
	all *paid staff?*	all *volunteers?*	
No use of office office technology for personal business	Yes	No	Add technology policy to volunteer handbook.
No personal or intimate relationships with clients	No	No	Make explicit by adding to both handbooks, and orientation agenda.
Only designated staff may transport clients in personal vehicles	No	Yes	Add driving restriction to employee handbook and discuss at next staff meeting.
All staff must attend the twice annual safety briefing	No	No	Convene safety briefing ASAP to discuss procedures and new policy.

Fix the Fixable

If you were to ask a typical nonprofit manager if there is something going on in the organization that could "blow up" in the organization's face and cause a crisis, most managers would be able to identify something pretty quickly, such as:

- "Our bookkeeper is incompetent and I'm worried about all of the mistakes he's been making lately."

- "We've got a staff member who likes to send angry letters to the editors of major newspapers about controversial topics."

- "Fifty percent of our grant funding comes from one source and it's likely that the grant won't be renewed at the end of the month."

From the bizarre to the truly frightening almost every imaginable response to the question posed above is one that begs for a fix. If that's the case with your potential crisis, fix it. Replace the bookkeeper with someone capable of doing the job (following all of your established employment practices, of course, and consult legal counsel before terminating the staff member). Meet with the staff member to review your technology policy and prohibition on using the nonprofit's equipment to express personal views (or update your policy so that it explicitly prohibits such acts). Begin work immediately on downsizing your organization so you can operate with 50 percent of your prior revenue stream.

Use Available Trends and Data

For predicting the cause or source of the next preventable crisis, every nonprofit has access to a crystal-ball-like tool: history. Include your nonprofit's history, as well as the history and experiences of the nonprofits in the world in which you live (advocacy groups, social services providers, cultural organizations, religious organizations). Take a look at what's happened in the past and consider whether that crisis (death of your executive director, loss of major grant funding, fire at your facility) could happen again.

Once your crisis management plan is in place, you'll be in a strong position to use historical information since you'll be documenting any crisis that occurs and conducting an assessment of what happened and what's required to prevent the crisis from re-occurring. In the meantime, take a look at your history and consider the history of similar organizations.

Get Help

Every nonprofit needs outside professional help from time to time. Whether it's analyzing past workplace accidents or developing legally sound employment practices, few organizations have the inside resources to go it alone. And in so many cases, an "outsider's" views can be invaluable to putting your situation in perspective.

Don't be shy about asking for help in order to get your nonprofit back on a healthy track or to fix persistent problems that could cause lasting damage if ignored.

Look Before you Leap

"Consult your physician before beginning any new exercise regimen." This warning, resulting from the fear of legal liability, appears on all advertisementd for nutritional supplements, diet pills, exercise videos or equipment, and even devices that stimulate muscle movement and allow the user to get "rock hard abs" without having to exercise at all. In the context of preventing a crisis in a nonprofit organization, this advice might turn out to be good medicine. Every nonprofit has a certain comfort zone when it comes to service and program delivery. If you're a day care center for children, you have expertise in providing care for young children. The decision to add adult day care as a new service presents a new set of risks for your organization. Proceed with caution and deliberate motion as you consider these risks. If you're a literacy program operating at the public library, the decision to provide one-to-one mentoring outside the library environment means you've got some new risks to evaluate.

As we indicated earlier, every nonprofit must take risks to accomplish its mission. Crisis management isn't about eliminating risks or avoiding them altogether. But when you're stepping into unfamiliar territory, you need to take the time required to consider what you're getting into, identify the hurdles and plan how you can rid yourself of them or leap high enough to land on the other side unscathed and in one piece.

Use Common Sense

Participants in training events sponsored by the Nonprofit Risk Management Center often seem surprised to discover that integrating risk management in a nonprofit often boils down to applying common sense in a thoughtful, consistent way. If there is a "Wizard of Oz" behind the curtain of risk management, it's the voice and face of reason: Use common sense. Whether you're working to prevent a financial catastrophe or prevent client maltreatment, always factor in what makes practical sense for your nonprofit. Don't establish goals or rules that can't be practically implemented by your workforce. Don't focus all of your energies on preventing a lawsuit alleging sexual harassment when the most likely cause of crisis in your nonprofit is the nonrenewal of your public funding.

Phase 3:   **Surviving a Crisis**

Acknowledge the Problem

"Houston, we have a problem." Recognizing a problem exists is the first step to addressing it. Acknowledging you're facing a crisis is the first step in getting your nonprofit back on track and focusing all of your energy on an important, community-serving mission. There's almost no point in having a plan to deal with a crisis if you refuse to acknowledge you're facing one.

Individuals in your organization have different perceptions of when a crisis is at hand. Most nonprofits have at least one alarmist who perceives the depletion of the coffee supply to be disastrous. On the other hand, the always cool-as-a-cucumber type will stop to gather personal items and respond to an e-mail as the sound of the fire alarm echoes through the building. Most nonprofit managers fall somewhere in between these extremes. They recognize that while day-to-day existence in a nonprofit organization can be stressful, and at times unpredictable, they know a real crisis when they see it.

Don't be the last to see that you're facing a crisis. Keep your eyes open for the signs of a crisis so that all of the planning and preparation undertaken has the best chance of doing some good. Keep in mind that perception is or may become reality. Groucho Marx asked, "Are you going to believe what you see or what I'm telling you?" What a client or other constituent "sees" or believes they see may soon be your reality. So if a client perceives your facilities to be unsafe, or an employee believes she has been the victim of racial discrimination, you may have a crisis on your hands. Also remember that a crisis can slither up on you like a python, or attack suddenly and without warning like a cobra. It's not always easy to see it coming.

Call in the Troops

Follow the plan. Locate the list and contact the crisis team members. Once the team is assembled, the team leader should brief them on the situation. During this important, initial overview the team leader should try to answer the following questions:

❑ What has happened? What event has occurred or what problem was uncovered?

❑ Who has been affected thus far by the events? Who are the known victims?

❑ What steps have been taken thus far to control the crisis? Who has done what?

❑ Is the media aware of the crisis? Are we ready to give a statement?

The team should discuss, and quickly and carefully decide, what actions need to be taken to:

- provide/arrange care or support for victims;

- arrange for financing or take other action to replenish cash;

- notify key partners, such as the nonprofit's legal counsel and insurance professional;

- respond to media inquiries;

- brief the paid and volunteer staff of the organization;

- brief key constituents of the organization;

- assure continued service delivery or coordinate transfer of clients/services to another provider;

- secure any important documents, computer backups, etc.;

- validate that communications systems are in place and operational.

Assignments should then be made for each critical task, and the team should identify a time and location to reconvene and reassess the situation. Depending on the nature of the crisis, this may be every few hours, once a day or less frequently.

Keep Constituents in the Loop

Communication is an important component of the handling of a crisis. How an organization communicates with key constituents, responds to inquiries and criticism, and tells its story may be the single largest determinant of its survival. A failed communications strategy can spell disaster for even a large and mature organization.

During a crisis, it's essential that you communicate with affected constituencies. Part of your crisis management plan is to identify and rank these audiences. Some of these may be readily apparent, such as clients to whom you can no longer provide services, the parents or guardians of young clients, staff members, volunteers and the nonprofit's board of directors. Other key constituencies may be less apparent, such as funders, donors, organizations providing similar services in the community, or the local government where the nonprofit operates.

You will undoubtedly need to communicate with the persons serving as professional advisors to your nonprofit. Reaching the following individuals should be an early priority: legal counsel, financial advisors and your insurance professional.

Remember to alert constituencies who may not know about the crisis until you tell them. Consider whether it's important for any of these groups to be informed about the crisis: public and private funders, and local/state regulatory agencies.

Basic Rules for Crisis Communications

Any communication during a crisis should be carefully orchestrated. Whether communication is directed at an internal or external audience and whether it is written, verbal or visual, organizations should take extra care in crafting messages during a crisis. The topic of crisis communications is well documented and various books are available on this subset of crisis management. Authors Mike Stephen and Stephen Moore in their book, *Effective Crisis Management*, urge organizations to apply the "Five Cs" to every crisis communication:

1. ***Care*** — The public is reluctant to forgive lack of compassion from an organization whose services or programs form the backdrop for harm. Nowhere is this truer than in the nonprofit sector. Nonprofits are perceived as being in the compassion business. An effective spokesperson for a nonprofit is someone who can express empathy and caring with conviction and sincerity. A nonprofit representative who is communicating in a crisis must be able to convey the organization's deep concern about the situation and empathy for victims. This has practical importance, as well. Many plaintiffs pursue a legal remedy because they believe the organization whose actions, inactions or activities caused harm didn't care about their injuries or losses. The most effective way to ward off a lawsuit is by expressing care and concern.

2. ***Commitment*** — The second element of crisis communications is commitment. The nonprofit's message should resound that the organization is committed to investigating the incident and preventing further occurrences.

3. ***Consistency*** — A clear plan of how an organization will respond and what its spokesperson will say, assures a consistent message will be communicated to the public. Some listeners will be suspicious when the organization's message is inconsistent, believing that the organization's leadership doesn't have its act together or that someone is lying or covering up the truth.

4. ***Coherence*** — It's important to be clear and concise. Say what you need to say and no more. Rambling on just creates confusion and raises the chance that you will try to say what you think the audience wants to hear rather than sticking to the facts and the message *you* want to communicate.

5. ***Clarity*** — The opportunity to convey a message may come without warning, and it's likely to be a small window. Use the time to convey vital information. Avoid jargon and other language that will confuse the listener. A good test of the content is to ask yourself:

What do I want the listener to think of the organization at the end of my statement?

Key Documents in a Crisis Communications Strategy

❑ *The Summary Statement* — The summary statement is a valuable piece of your crisis communications strategy. It allows you to communicate what you know quickly. The statement explains what happened, describes what your nonprofit is doing, and expresses how the organization feels. Authors Stephen and Moore stress that the statement be compassionate without being "mawkish, defensive, trite or insincere." Craft the statement carefully, keeping in mind that the media may extract from it one or two phrases that could appear out of context in print or on a Web site, or be incorporated into television or radio stories.

Summary Statement

ABC Nonprofit learned early this morning that 20 members of the Pleasantville community that is serves were taken to a hospital emergency room complaining of nausea, headache and fever. Executive Director Joseph E. Brown has spoken with all the afflicted people, many of whom eat at ABC each day.

Mr. Brown and his staff are reviewing their procedures to make certain that ABC's food handling protocols for serving nutritious food safely have been followed to the letter.

❑ *Q & A Fact Sheet* — One of the first tasks in the execution of your crisis communications plan should be the development of a fact sheet in a Q & A format. It should generally address what happened and who's responsible, provide an assessment of the danger of a situation, and describe in clear terms what the organization is doing about the situation. The information should be short and to-the-point. Avoid jargon or, if that's not possible, explain jargon in lay terms. Update the information as the crisis unfolds and new developments occur. The fact sheet should include the kinds of questions the organization has been asked to date and ones anticipated in the future. The fact sheet will be an important guide for your spokesperson, who should review it carefully. Sticking to the information on the fact sheet is the best way to ensure that your spokesperson is prepared to respond effectively and consistently to questions. A sample Q & A fact sheet appears on the next page.

❑ *Media Kit* — A media kit provides background on your organization. Think of it as a two-minute education on the who, what, when, where, why and how of your nonprofit's mission, governance, funding, clientele, staff and board members. Ideally,

SAMPLE

Fact Sheet
ABC Nonprofit
1445 Central Avenue
Pleasantville, IL 30000
P: (333) 222-0000
Contact: Joseph E. Brown

Q: *What is ABC Nonprofit?*
A: ABC Nonprofit, founded in 1945, is dedicated to providing nourishing meals to the residents of Pleasantville who have no other means of receiving food.

Q: *How many people does ABC Nonprofit serve each year?*
A: ABC Nonprofit feeds, on average, 10,000 people per year.

Q: *Who funds ABC Nonprofit?*
A: ABC Nonprofit receives funds from the United Giving Campaign in the community. Food and beverages are donated by hotels, catering firms and restaurants in the city and surrounding communities. Local corporations sponsor individual events. Individual donations are welcome.

Q: *How does ABC Nonprofit ensure that the food it serves is safe?*
A: The businesses that donate food to ABC's program employ professional food handlers, who are educated in safe food handling. ABC's corporate partners have provided commercial freezers, refrigerators and ranges for the kitchens and a safe food handling protocol for staff and volunteers.

Q: *Why did 20 people who ate at ABC's downtown location get salmonella?*
A: ABC is seeking the answer to that question. ABC has protocols and a training program in place for all staff and volunteers who handle food served to the public. We are committed to providing nourishing food in a safe environment for the people of Pleasantville who are unable to receive food from other sources.

these materials have been written in electronic form and updated as the information changes. Thus, when a crisis strikes, all you need do is print them out. Oops! What if the network malfunctions? Better have copies in your crisis management manual just in case. To this basic background, you can add the summary statement and Q & A Fact Sheet about the current situation.

❑ *Media Contact Strategy* — If your crisis has attracted the attention of the media, you need to create a plan to keep the media informed of developments. This keeps your nonprofit in control — to the extent possible — of the flow of information about the crisis. Deadlines drive the media. If you're dealing with two or three outlets (i.e., local radio, television and newspaper reporters), you can call and update them on an hourly basis, or as new information becomes available. If you're dealing with more outlets or a story of national or international import, you can hold a news conference to which you invite interested parties. You arrange for your spokesperson to present at one time to all reporters with a Q & A session to follow. Major developments can be handled in follow-up briefings. These group presentations reduce the wear and tear on your spokesperson and experts, and all media outlets receive the same information at the same time. Ideally, you will have a media contact list prepared and updated on a regular basis. A copy of this will be in your Crisis Management Manual. You might also find a media strategy checklist, such as the one on the next page, helpful to keep you on track in the swirl of activity.

Understand the Media

A good starting point in dealing effectively with the media during a crisis is to try to appreciate the ability of the media to play a crucial role in your crisis. It's also helpful to understand the motivations and agenda of the media. With respect to their interest in your crisis, generally speaking, media representatives will be looking for an engaging story, trying to determine the cause of the crisis, and hoping to identify the heroes and villains in the story. Much of how they respond to, react to and report a story will result from the non-negotiable deadlines of the business.

Media outlets compete to be the first to report a story, and reporters are under constant deadline pressure. Few have the luxury of reporting a story only after all the facts have come out. So it's important to understand that your story — if it's the type that would engage reader, listener or viewer interest — *will be reported*, with or without your assistance. It's rarely wise to refuse to cooperate with the media or to say, "no comment." It sounds bad and many will assume that you are hiding something. However, there are questions you won't want to answer because of how they are phrased. The age-old example is "When did you stop beating your wife?" You can always choose not to directly answer a reporter's question, and instead deliver the message you want the public to hear. In the case of the age-old example, your answer, stated in an even tone with a smile, might be "I'm a bachelor," or "I don't beat my wife or anyone, for that matter." And a word to the wise, there is no such thing as "off the record." If you say it, it's fair game.

Many resources are available on media relations. Some of the most practical and potentially valuable advice from experts in the field includes the following:

- ❑ *Be clear about what you want the media to know.* You control what you tell them about the organization and the incident.

- ❑ *Always tell the truth.* Mike Seymour and Simon Moore in their book, *Effective Crisis Management*, call this advice the critical "Three Ts" of crisis communications (Tell The Truth).

- ❑ *Don't feel that you need to tell the media everything you know.* In fact, it may be dangerous to do so, since you then give the reporter the chance to pick the sound bite that will air — and it may be a phrase or comment that hurts you when taken out of context.

❑ Where possible, *stick to the prepared text.* The written documents in your communications strategy are essential tools for surviving media interviews. Think of your fact sheet as more than a list of talking points; it's, essentially, your script.

❑ *If you don't know, say so.* If feasible, agree to try to find the answer and indicate you'll get back to the reporter.

❑ *Don't be a cynic, be sincere.* The resident cynic in your office may not be your most effective media spokesperson. Choose someone who is comfortably and convincingly sincere.

Media Contact Log

Date/ Time	Reporter's Name	Organization	Telephone	Handled by
2/5/02 2:30 pm	Inquiring Iris	Action News	(202) 555-5555	Elizabeth
2/5/02 3:00 pm	Pesky Pete	Need to Know News	(703) 555-5555	Elizabeth

Media Strategy Checklist

Task	Completed? Yes	No
Alert the spokesperson.	■	❑
Gather the who, what, where, when and why of the situation.	■	❑
Confirm the facts.	❑	■
Clarify and verify technical information.	❑	■
Prepare a summary statement.	■	❑
Prepare a fact sheet.	❑	■
Notify people key to the nonprofit.	❑	■
Tell volunteers and clients about changes in services/operations.	❑	■
Respond to media.	❑	■
Keep a media log of callers and questions.	❑	■
Update media as situation develops.	❑	■
Follow up implications; prevent backlash.	❑	■
Evaluate and tweak the system.	❑	■

❑ *Accommodate reasonable requests.* On occasion a reporter will make a special request, such as requesting that an introduction to a news piece be taped in front of your organization's entry, or an interview be held at the location of an incident rather than in an office. If it's possible to accommodate a special request without jeopardizing your crisis communications plan, be cooperative.

❑ *Admit when a mistake has been made.* In some cases admitting that a mistake has been made is the first step to re-establishing credibility and confidence with key constituencies.

❑ *Don't ignore requests from the media or evade interviews.* Playing hide-'n'-seek has the potential to cause a great deal of harm, as the reporter you're avoiding will try to find *someone* to speak to about the situation. Someone almost always surfaces and it's possible that person won't be an effective representative of your organization or position. Why put the selection of a spokesperson in the hands of a potentially uninformed reporter?

❑ *Designate a backup for your spokesperson in the event your spokesperson is unavailable or is the subject of the crisis.* Both the spokesperson and the backup should be trained, articulate, sincere and persuasive.

How to deal with the media is important, needless to say. However, it's also important to consider the vital and long-term audience for the organization. Who matters to the organization? Who does your organization matter to?

Record What's Done

Record keeping is probably the last thing on your mind in the middle of a crisis, but your attorney, insurance professional and board will bless you many times over if you track the key stages and responsive actions by your crisis management team. One driving need for good records documenting the event is the possibility that a lawsuit will ensue. Written records made on the scene as the action is occurring are much more powerful one or two years after the event, than individual memories. The written record will be less likely to be called into question or manipulated by a clever opposing attorney with visions of dollars signs in his eyes.

Keep a record of who contacted whom for your files on the handling of each crisis. A sample appears on the next page.

Remain Flexible

The crisis management team performs as a trauma team. Think of the TV show, "M*A*S*H." Each of the doctors had a medical degree, which represents knowledge and training. The battlefield required

Crisis Activities Log

ABC Nonprofit

Describe the Crisis (who, what, when, where, why?) _____

_____

_____

Date	Time	Action / By whom?
2/5/02	1:30 pm	Mary received a bomb threat from an anonymous caller.
2/5/02	1:35 pm	Steve began evacuating the building.
2/5/02	1:35 pm	Mary called 911, using a wireless phone in the parking lot.
2/5/02	1:40 pm	The police and fire departments arrived at ABC Nonprofit.
2/5/02	1:45 pm	Joanne began calling parents to request that they pick up their children as soon as possible.
2/5/02	2:30 pm	A Need to Know News crew arrived and interviewed Elizabeth Spokesperson for the 6:00 pm broadcast.

they take their skills and apply them in unknown conditions in life-or-death situations. They improvised. They kept moving and evaluating. You can do just the same when a crisis hits your nonprofit.

Keep a cool head. Analyze the situation as it unfolds. Remain open to change. Your Crisis Management Manual is a guide to help you think through steps in the midst of chaos. You have outlined scenarios for the most likely probabilities, but life happens and it's not predictable. Refer to the closest scenario you have in your Crisis Management Manual. Skim the checklist. Then consult your crisis management team and modify as needed.

Close the Loop

If your organization has anticipated a crisis and established plans to manage or respond to events, you'll obviously be in a better position to repair the damage and move forward. The nature of activities that should be undertaken during the survival phase vary based on the causes and manifestations of the crisis. Was the crisis the result of human error or a natural disaster? Was there any warning that the organization was going to be embroiled in a crisis?

With wide variation due to the circumstances at hand, the resolution phase generally encompasses efforts to:

❑ Make those who were injured whole by providing financial assistance or other support.

❑ Restore or replace damaged, lost or stolen property.

❑ Maintain or resume critical operations as quickly as possible.

❑ Communicate continually with staff, board members, clients and the media to keep them updated on what the organization is doing in response to the crisis and restore or sustain confidence in the organization.

Debrief Participants

Under certain circumstances, particularly where key constituents of your nonprofit have suffered trauma, a psychological debriefing such as the Critical Incident Stress Debriefing developed by Jeffrey T. Mitchell, Ph.D., may be a required in the aftermath of a crisis. Prior partnerships with other organizations can be very useful in this situation. You will need the assistance of experts. According to the book *Critical Incident Stress Management*, Second Edition, by George S. Everly, Jr. and Jeffrey T. Mitchell, CISD refers to a specific "seven-stage group crisis intervention technique."

CISD, which Mitchell originally developed from the late 1970s through mid-'80s, has been adapted and used by rescue, disaster and health-care groups in various settings, businesses and industries.

The seven-stage technique is used to "bring psychological closure" to homogeneous groups of victims or witnesses after a "traumatic event." Thus, it isn't used repeatedly throughout an event, nor will it be used during an ongoing event. Ideally, the intervention occurs 24 hours after the end of their involvement. Realistically, these debriefings are held one to 10 days after an "acute crisis" and three to four weeks after a "mass disaster."

CISD aims to reduce the negative impact from a traumatic incident by taking the participants through seven stages: Introduction, Fact, Thought, Reaction, Symptom, Teaching and Re-entry. Each participant voluntarily describes an incident that happened, his or her reaction to the incident and its psychological impact; and learns how to manage stress. You will need to hire a professional to facilitate the CISD process.

Evaluate the Response

As a crisis subsides, one of the key tasks of the crisis response team is to evaluate the organization's response and the overall effectiveness of the action plan. Incorporating lessons learned during a crisis and adjusting the action plan for future events ensures that the organization — and its key personnel — learns from its experience. Earlier in this book we stated that one of the few certainties in a crisis is that one or more lessons will be learned. It's not too early during the cooling off or winding down stages of a crisis to start documenting these lessons and determining how they can make the nonprofit stronger and more capable and confident in responding to future events.

It's also important to evaluate what you did during the crisis. Consider:

- ❑ What happened?

- ❑ What were the major causes of the crisis?

- ❑ How soon did the organization recognize and respond to the crisis?

- ❑ Were staff, board members and others who were involved and/or affected informed in a timely fashion?

- ❑ Did the media learn of the crisis? How effectively did the organization respond to media inquiries?

- ❑ How effective was the crisis response team? Were any needed skills or talents missing in the make-up of the team?

- ❑ How well did the team follow the action plan?

- ❑ How effective and useful was the plan?

- ❑ What could have been done better or differently?

- ❑ Does the plan need to be changed? If so, in what way?

- ❑ Was prompt contact made with outside resources, such as police, fire department, ambulance, insurance companies, lawyers and those whose help was needed during the crisis?

In addition to looking at everything that went right during the crisis, there are lots of potential lessons in what — if anything — went wrong. Remember that many successful individuals and organizations have emerged from failure. Ray Kroc abandoned a failed attempt at selling real estate before he began selling hamburgers. The founders of Sony, who failed at their first business, went on to found an electronics giant. Entrepreneurs and entrepreneurial organizations are often those that learn from their missteps.

Revise the Crisis Plan

Whatever glitches you've discovered in handling the last crisis need to be remedied and incorporated into your crisis management plan and reflected in the Crisis Management Manual. With the team's self-evaluations in hand, talk with them and assign tasks and deadlines to improve things that didn't work, strengthen what did work and streamline the cumbersome.

Self-assessment Worksheet
(Crisis Response Team)

This worksheet can be completed as a group effort by the team working together, or individually by each team member.

What Happened? _____

Major Causes? _____

Time Line (recognition to response to end) _____

How soon was the board informed about the crisis?
❑ within hours ❑ within 24 hours ❑ within a week
❑ never, because _____

Did the media learn of the crisis? ❑ Yes ❑ No
How? _____

How effectively did the organization respond to media inquiries?
❑ very effectively ❑ somewhat effectively ❑ ineffectively

How effective was the crisis response team?
❑ highly effective ❑ effective ❑ marginally effective

What, if any, skills or talents were missing in the make-up of the team?

Did the team follow the action plan? If not, what were the deviations and why? Should these deviations be incorporated into a revised plan?

Did the plan work? What could be done more effectively/efficiently and how?

Does the plan need to be changed in other ways? How?

Was prompt contact made with outside resources, such as police, fire, ambulance, insurance companies, lawyers and those whose help was needed during the crisis?

Train Staff and Volunteers

When the plan is rewritten, communicate it to your constituents and incorporate the changes into the next training session. Also make certain that you've folded the changes into the drills for staff, volunteers and clients. In this case practice doesn't make perfect. Practice prepares participants to think "crisis management" when the crisis hits. The drills set the tone for proactive, resourceful, targeted actions geared at reducing the impact and saving the nonprofit so that it can continue to deliver services to the community.

Heal Thyself

Once an organization puts its crisis management strategy into play, notifies constituencies and prevents the situation from snowballing, it's time to focus on creating a lasting solution to the root causes of the crisis.

For example, if the crisis was caused by the theft of the nonprofit's financial assets or property by an insider, the healing process requires focus on preventing a similar theft from occurring in the future. It's time to bring together a team of individuals with expertise in internal controls who can assist the nonprofit's senior managers to fashion a practical system that dissuades would-be embezzlers and ensures that fraud is detected as quickly as possible.

If mistreatment or alleged mistreatment of a young participant caused the crisis, then the healing process should focus on a range of issues, including scrutinizing the organization's strategies for screening, selecting and supervising staff.

If the crisis was caused by the inability to access facilities following a natural disaster, the process should address the effectiveness of the organization's contingency plans for continuing service delivery and using backup materials stored offsite to recreate files and databases. The point here is to identify the source of the problem and make systemic changes that will prevent the same thing from recurring. As embarrassing as a crisis can be, a preventable crisis that happens twice is not bad luck. It's mismanagement.

Epilogue

This Too Shall Pass

Perhaps you will be fortunate and never have to manage an organization in crisis during your career. In all likelihood you won't escape that experience. Yet, the odds are in your favor that you will prevail and that the organization will survive and go on to thrive. You can improve these odds by anticipating and preparing for the crisis, by proactively managing the situation with calm and compassion, and by learning from mistakes and moving on.

If, as you are reading these words, the future seems bright, it may be hard to imagine that anything could cause a major disruption to your mission or the services you provide to your community. On the other hand, if a crisis has already erupted in your organization, you may wonder if the nonprofit will ever return to a sound footing. There are perhaps two sentiments that are equally unproductive. They are unwarranted confidence and unbridled despair. Before succumbing to either, take a deep breath and repeat to yourself: This too shall pass.

Bibliography and Resources

Bibliography

Books

Bram, Alan and Jill Maidhof, *Crisis Management Manual*, Jewish Community Campus of Greater Kansas City, Overland Park, Kan.

Everly, George S. Jr. and Jeffrey T. Mitchell, *Critical Incident Stress Management: CISM, A New Era and Standard of Care in Crisis Intervention*, Second Edition, Chevron Publishing Corp., Ellicott City, Md., 1999.

Harvard Business Review on Crisis Management, Harvard Business Review School Publishing, Boston, 2000.

Hauge, Jennifer Chandler and Melanie L. Herman, *Taking the High Road: A Guide to Effective and Legal Employment Practices for Nonprofits*, Nonprofit Risk Management Center, Washington, D.C., 1999.

Meyers, Gerald C. and Susan Meyers, *Dealers, Healers, Brutes & Saviors: Eight Winning Styles for Solving Giant Business Crises*, John Wiley & Sons Inc., New York, 2000.

Patterson, John and Pamela Rypkema, *Crisis Management for Nonprofit Organizations: Ten Steps for Survival*, Nonprofit Risk Management Center, Washington, D.C., 1996.

Schwartz, Alan M. and Fred Hetner, *Security for Community Institutions: A Handbook*, Fourth Edition, Anti-Defamation League, New York, 1999.

Seymour, Mike and Simon Moore, *Effective Crisis Management: Worldwide Principles and Practice*, Cassell, London, New York, 2000.

Articles from Magazines, Newsletters and Online Publications

"Crime Prevention for Small Businesses," National Crime Prevention Council
    See www.ncpc.org/1smbus.htm

"Crisis Definitions," Institute for Crisis Management, 2000.
    See www.crisisexperts.com/crisisdefinitions.htm

"Crisis Preparedness Questions For Your Next Management Meeting," Institute for Crisis Management, 2000.
    See www.crisisexperts.com/prepare.htm

"Evangelical Lutherans: Ex-Treasurer Accused of Embezzlement," *Christianity Today*,
Vol. 40, No. 13, Nov. 11, 1996, pg. 103b.
See www.christianityonline.com/ct/6td/6td03b.html

"Former Episcopal Church Treasurer Begins Prison Sentence for Embezzlement."
Episcopal News Service, August 1996.
See www.dfms.org/ens/cookeint.html

"Foundation for New Era Philanthropy Founder Will Use 'Religious Fervor' Defense at
Trial," *Philanthropy News Digest*, Vol. 3, Issue 10, March 12,1997.
See http://fdncenter.org/pnd/19970312/001416.html

Freeo, Sandra K. Clawson, "Crisis Communication Plan: A Blue Print for Crisis
Communication," Northern Illinois University's Newsplace for News and
Sources.
See http://publicrelations.about.com/gi/dynamic/offsite.htm

Ging, Tim, "Good Communications In Bad Situations," *Contingency Planning &
Management*, Vol. II, No.6, June 1997, pgs. 14-16.

Goldstein, Henry, "In Scandals, Don't Let Boards off the Hook," *The Chronicle of
Philanthropy*, October 1996. Reprinted by the Oram Group.
See www.oramgroup.com/pubs.html

"Groups in Foundation for New Era Philanthropy Case to Recover $61 Million,"
Philanthropy News Digest, Vol. 3, Issue 30, July 30, 1997.
See http://fdncenter.org/pnd/19970730/001646.html

Hamilton, Dennis C., "Concepts of Crisis Management."
See www.crpc.com

Hamilton, Dennis C., "Crisis Management: Case Study."
See www.crpc.com

Hamilton, Dennis C., "Evaluation and Selection of Commercial Technology Based
Recovery Services," 1998.
See www.crpc.com

Hamilton, Dennis C., "Multilateral Continuity Planning Concepts."
See www.crpc.com

"Hazard maps help save lives and property," (U.S. Geological Survey Fact Sheet-183-96)
U.S. Geological Survey, 1996.
See http://quake.wr.usgs.gov/QUAKES/FactSheets/RiskMaps

Irvine, Robert B. and Dan P. Millar, "Debunking the Stereotypes of Crisis Management:
The Nature of Business Crisis in the 1990's." (A Paper Presented at: The 5th
Annual Conference on Crisis Management, University of Nevada at Las Vegas,
Aug. 8, 1996).
See www.crisisexperts.com/pub.htm

Irvine, Robert B. and Dan P. Millar, "Multiplying The Effects: Factors Influencing Media
Coverage of Business Crises," (A Paper Presented at the 6th Annual Conference
on Crisis Management, University of Nevada at Las Vegas, Aug. 7, 1997).
See www.crisisexperts.com/pub.htm

"Is crisis counseling available?" Federal Emergency Management Agency, Recovery and
Response, May 21, 1999.
See www.fema.gov/r-n-r/counsel.htm

Jones, David R., "Crisis management: when bad things happen to good organizations," *The Nonprofit Times*. November 1997, 1:54.

Klein, Wendy, "Embezzlement: Some of the Best Employees Have Done It," Aug. 23-29, 1999. *See* www.ec2.edu/dccenter/sba/082399.html

Mullen, Jennifer, "Community Relations Strategies Are Necessary for Nonprofit Organizations," *NRCCSA News*, Vol. 5, No.1, January/February 1996, pgs. 4-5, The National Resource Center on Child Sexual Abuse.

"New Era Chief Diverted Funds," *Philanthropy News Digest,* Vol. 1, Issue 22, June 7, 1995. *See* http://fdncenter.org/pnd/19950607/000340.html

"New Era Philanthropy Founder John G. Bennett Jr. Sentenced to 12 Years in Prison," *Philanthropy News Digest,* Vol. 3, Issue 38, Sept. 24, 1997. *See* http://fdncenter.org/pnd/19970924/001739.html

"New Era Trustee Asks Charities to Return Funds," *Philanthropy News Digest,* Vol. 1, Issue 21, May 31, 1995. *See* http://fdncenter.org/pnd/19950531/000326.html

Nordboe, Diana, "Crisis Counseling Assistance and Training Program: Best Practices Document," Center for Mental Health Services, January 2000. *See* www.mentalhealth.org/cmhs/EmergencyServices/Esdrb/index.htm

Rudolph, Barbara, "Coping With Catastrophe: Crisis Management Becomes the New Corporate Discipline," *TIME Magazine*, Feb. 24, 1986. *See* www.crisismanagement.com/time.html

"Scandals: A Close Look at Scandals in the Nonprofit Sector," A special edition of *Board Member*, Vol. 5, No. 5, National Center for Nonprofit Boards, Washington, D.C., September 1996.

"SEC Settles Lawsuit Against Foundation for New Era Philanthropy Founder," *Philanthropy News Digest,* Vol. 4, Issue 6, Feb. 11, 1998. *See* http://fdncenter.org/pnd/19980211/001936.html

Simonelli, Mitchelle, "Lasting Effects: The Human Dimension of Disaster Recovery," *Contingency Planning & Management*, May/June 2000, pgs. 36-39.

Smith, Michael, *Crisis Communication: A textbook for a workshop on crisis management,* Nonprofit Management Development Center at LaSalle University School of Business Administration, Philadelphia, 2000.

Steinberg, Jacob and Jodi Wills, "Emotional Rescue," *Contingency Planning & Management*, Vol. II, No.5, May 1997, pgs. 27-30.

"Suffered a (natural) Disaster?" eMag Solutions, 1999. *See* www.emaglink.com/tmm/disaster.html

"Supreme Court Refuses to Hear Foundation for New Era Philanthropy," *Philanthropy News Digest,* Vol. 5, Issue 40, Oct. 5, 1999. *See* http://fdncenter.org/pnd/19991005/002945.html

"The Essence of Crisis Management," Institute for Crisis Management, 2000. *See* www.crisisexperts.com/essence.htm

Resources

The bimonthly magazine *Contingency Planning & Management* has a variety of helpful resources. Although the magazine targets corporations, it often contains information that may be useful in a nonprofit environment. *Contingency Planning & Management* is a publication of Witter Publishing Corporation. Qualified subscribers get a free copy of the magazine. Nonqualified subscription rates are $99 per year in the United States and Canada and $150 for subscribers in all other countries.

Contingency Planning & Management
84 Park Avenue
Flemington, NJ 08822
Phone: (908) 788-0343
Fax: (908) 788-3782
www.contingencyplanning.com

A Web site *Earthquake Information: Reducing Hazards* is run by the U. S. Geological Survey and Geologic Division. U. S. Geological Survey is a bureau of the Department of the Interior. This Web site provides information on recent earthquakes, as well as information on earthquake and hazard preparedness.

U. S. Geological Survey, MS 977
345 Middlefield Road
Menlo Park, CA 94025
Earthquake Information Hotline (415) 329-4085
www.usgs.gov/index.html

The *Philanthropy News Digest* is provided by the Foundation Center in a digest form. PND covers philanthropy-related articles and is posted to the Foundation Center's Web site weekly on Tuesday afternoon.

The Foundation Center
79 Fifth Avenue
New York, NY 10003
Phone: (212) 620-4230
Fax: (212) 691-1828
http://fdncenter.org/pnd/current/index.html

The *Disaster Resource Guide* is published annually and provides the reader with the latest trends in crisis management and useful tips, as well as companies that provide products and services for information technology recovery, contingency management planning and more.

Emergency Lifeline Corp.
P.O. Box 15243
Santa Ana, CA 92735
Phone: (714) 558-8940
Fax: (714) 558-8901
www.disaster-resource.com

The *RiskList Resource for Risk Managers* has a variety of resources on risk management available on the Internet. Information is listed by category and these categories may help you determine what you have to consider.
http://home.clara.net/rlowther/risklist.html

Government agencies, organizations and institutions

The **Federal Emergency Management Agency** is a federal agency that is authorized and responsible for disaster relief, in cooperation with state/local agencies and nonprofit organizations. FEMA also provides various resources and tips to prevent or minimize damages caused by a disaster.

Hotline for crisis counseling, 1-800-525-0321 (TTY 1-800-462-7585)
www.fema.gov

The **Center for Mental Health Services** is under the U.S. Department of Health and Human Services. CMHS provides information and programs regarding mental health. The center's Crisis Counseling Assistance and Training Program was launched by the "Disaster Relief Act Amendment of 1974" (PL 93-288).

Center for Mental Health Services
P. O. Box 42490
Washington, DC 20015
Phone: (800) 789-2647 (301) 443-9006 (TDD)
International Calls: (301) 443-1805
Fax: (301) 984-8796
www.mentalhealth.org/cmhs/index.htm

Known for accepting blood donations, the **American Red Cross** is an international nonprofit organization actively involved in disaster response and biomedical services, as well as health and safety services. ARC helps communities prepare, mitigate and respond, and recover from a disaster. You can search for an ARC chapter nearest you at www.redcross.org/where/where.html by entering a zip code.

www.redcross.org

The **Salvation Army** is an international nonprofit organization serving the United States and more than 100 countries abroad by providing social services. In the USA, their disaster response services are well-recognized. The Salvation Army helps the victims and community affected by a disaster by providing counseling, financial assistance, shelter, and donated materials.

USA National Headquarters
The Salvation Army
P. O. Box 269
Alexandria, VA 22313
Phone: (703) 684 5500
Fax: (703) 684 3478
www.salvationarmyusa.org
www.salvationarmy.org

Worksheets

Inventory of Assets Worksheet

Create an inventory of your agency's possessions. Assign a person to record new items and to delete discarded items. Keep a copy of this inventory off-site in a fireproof box or a bank lock-box.

Asset Type: **Computer Equipment** (CPUs, monitors, file servers, universal power supply units, scanners, printers, storage devices, laptops, LCD projectors, cameras, etc.)

Name	Brand	Model	Serial #	Lessor	Lease #	Location	Date

Asset Type: **Furniture** (desks, filing cabinets, chairs, computer workstations, etc.)

Description	Brand	Model/Style	Lessor	Lease #	Location	Date

Asset Type: **Office Equipment** (telephones, photocopier, fax machine, postage meter, etc.)

Name	Brand	Model	Serial #	Lessor	Lease #	Location	Date

Asset Type: **Other Equipment** (playground equipment, medical equipment etc.)

Asset Type: **Databases** (client, volunteer, funder databases, etc.)

Description	Location	Purchase	Date

Asset Type: **Documents** (leases, partnership agreements, etc.)

Description	Location

Avoidable Crisis Assessment (Level 1) Worksheet

Organization: _____

Type	Could It Happen Here? Yes No	If yes, how likely? (5=very likely; 3=it could; 1=not likely)	How bad would it be? (5=very bad, significant cost; 3=bad, moderate cost; 1=not so bad, minimal cost)
Financial difficulties			
Funding source dries up			
Consolidation or merger			
Loses interest in the cause			
Goes bankrupt			
Cash flow uneven			
Event/campaign proceeds less than anticipated			
Client maltreatment			
Sexual abuse			
By staff (paid or volunteer)			
By another client			
Physical abuse			
By staff or volunteer			
By another client			
Service or product failure			
Food Poisoning (food bank, special event)			
Other _____			
Accidents			
Slip, trip and fall by client or general public			
Fire			
Household-chemical spill			
Guilt by association			
Major scandal affects...			
One of our "partners"			
Our segment of the nonprofit "world," e.g. United Ways			
Workplace violence			
By employee			
By employee's significant other			
Employment dispute			
Allegation of discrimination			
Allegation of harassment			
Other _____			
Criminal conduct that would cause a crisis			
Theft by staff or volunteer			
Property/equipment theft			

Unavoidable Crisis Assessment (Level 2) Worksheet

Organization: _____

Unavoidable Risks	Applicable?	Frequency (5=very likely; 3=it could; 1=not likely)	Severity/Cost (5=very bad, significant cost; 3=bad, moderate cost; 1=not so bad, minimal cost)	TOTAL SCORE	Notes
Natural disasters Hurricane	❑ yes ❑ no				
Tornado	❑ yes ❑ no				
Windstorm	❑ yes ❑ no				
Hailstorm	❑ yes ❑ no				
Earthquake	❑ yes ❑ no				
Landslide (mudslide)	❑ yes ❑ no				
Flood	❑ yes ❑ no				
Fire (wildfire)	❑ yes ❑ no				
Other incidents Bomb threat	❑ yes ❑ no				
Fire	❑ yes ❑ no				
Utility failure/leak	❑ yes ❑ no				
Hazmat incident	❑ yes ❑ no				
Sudden death CEO	❑ yes ❑ no				
Board Chair	❑ yes ❑ no				
Client	❑ yes ❑ no				
Volunteer	❑ yes ❑ no				
Computer hacked	❑ yes ❑ no				
Significant equipment-theft or data loss	❑ yes ❑ no				
Hostage threat	❑ yes ❑ no				
Terrorism	❑ yes ❑ no				
Workplace violence	❑ yes ❑ no				
Other _____ _____	❑ yes ❑ no				
_____ _____	❑ yes ❑ no				
_____ _____	❑ yes ❑ no				

Financial Crisis HistoryGram

Organization: _____

Describe past financial crisis	Could it happen again?	Could we have prevented it?	How?	Have we done done this? If not, have we set a target date?
_____ _____ _____ _____ _____ _____ _____ _____	❑ Yes ❑ No	❑ Yes ❑ No	_____ _____ _____ _____ _____ _____ _____	❑ Yes ❑ No
_____ _____ _____ _____ _____ _____ _____ _____	❑ Yes ❑ No	❑ Yes ❑ No	_____ _____ _____ _____ _____ _____ _____	❑ Yes ❑ No
_____ _____ _____ _____ _____ _____ _____ _____	❑ Yes ❑ No	❑ Yes ❑ No	_____ _____ _____ _____ _____ _____	❑ Yes ❑ No

Contingency Planning Worksheet

Event or activity: _____

Possible Snags	Options	What needs to be done?	By whom?
1.			
2.			
3.			
4.			

Event or activity: _____

Possible Snags	Options	What needs to be done?	By whom?
1.			
2.			
3.			
4.			

Event or activity: _____

Possible Snags	Options	What needs to be done?	By whom?
1.			
2.			
3.			
4.			

Crisis Management Relationships Worksheet

List the needs your organization would having during a crisis. Identify the potential sources of help, and how the source could provide other assistance that would strengthen your ability to survive a crisis.

Type/Category of Crisis: _____

What do we need?	Who can provide?	Do we have an arrangement?	How does it help?	How else could it help?
_____	_____	❑ yes ❑ no	_____	_____
_____	_____		_____	_____
_____	_____	❑ yes ❑ no	_____	_____
_____	_____		_____	_____
_____	_____	❑ yes ❑ no	_____	_____
_____	_____		_____	_____
_____	_____	❑ yes ❑ no	_____	_____
_____	_____		_____	_____

Constituent Contact Worksheet

A current list of constituent contacts is important to the lifeblood of your nonoprofit. Rank them in order of importance. List ways to reach them. Assign who will reach them in a crisis. Keep copies of the list at home, at work and in your Crisis Management Manual.

Rank	People	Organization	Best Method	By Whom?
1.				
2.				
3.				
4.				

Crisis Action Overview Worksheet

Transfer the risks and total scores from the Crisis Assessment Worksheets.

Don't hold back. If you see a solution that requires more resources than you currently have or can afford, indicate what they are. These will form a wish list for donations, sponsorships and next year's budget process.

Crisis Risk	Total Score	Is This Risk Avoidable?	What should be done to keep this risk from happening?	If this risk happens, what should be done immediately?	Resources we need, but not available at present time.
		❑ Yes ❑ No			
		❑ Yes ❑ No			
		❑ Yes ❑ No			
		❑ Yes ❑ No			
		❑ Yes ❑ No			
		❑ Yes ❑ No			

Crisis Action Steps Worksheet

A. Brainstorm: What are all the steps needed to get from A to Z?

Suggested approach to brainstorming:
We brainstorm to get out all possible ideas.
1. *mention all ideas; the more ideas, the better.*
2. *repetition is okay; people are thinking about their ideas and may miss hearing an idea mentioned, thus they repeat it.*
3. *no discussion; no face-making, hisses, sighs, cheers, no judging of anyone's ideas. Appoint a recorder to write down all ideas large enough for everyone to see.*

B. Rank steps in order of priority #1, #2, #3.

(Break into groups of three to five people. Ask each group to decide the sequence of events necessary to accomplish the task. Have each group report back their conclusions. Have the recorder keep a second list showing the relationships the members find.)

C. List steps and notes.

(When sequence of steps varies, discuss and reach agreement. Recorder can note rationale for sequence next to the step – helpful when making adjustments later.)

D. Create a flowchart: visualize action.

(Put each step in a box and position boxes to show that step's relationship to subsequent and previous steps. For instance, if the step is to douse the fire with water and that action quenches the fire, that's the end. However, if water doesn't put out the fire, the next step would be to pull the fire alarm, and then get the people safely out of the building.)

E. Prepare safety checklist.

(Pull together a list of tips that people need to have as "ready reference" in this emergency.)

Record of Emergency Drills

Organization: _____

Nature of Drill: _____

Date/Time	Participants	Observations	Follow-up status
_____	_____	_____	_____
_____	_____	_____	_____
_____	_____	_____	_____

Staff Instructions Worksheet

To identify where weaknesses lie, develop a worksheet listing required staff behaviors at your nonprofit. Use the worksheet to evaluate whether adequate instruction has been provided and determine what additional follow-up is needed.

Required Behaviors	Adequate instruction provided to: all *paid staff*?	all *volunteers*?	Additional follow-up required
_____ _____	❑ Yes ❑ No	❑ Yes ❑ No	_____ _____
_____ _____	❑ Yes ❑ No	❑ Yes ❑ No	_____ _____
_____ _____	❑ Yes ❑ No	❑ Yes ❑ No	_____ _____

Media Strategy Checklist

Task	Completed? Yes	No
Alert the spokesperson.	❑	❑
Gather the who, what, where, when and why of the situation.	❑	❑
Confirm the facts.	❑	❑
Clarify and verify technical information.	❑	❑
Prepare a summary statement.	❑	❑
Prepare a fact sheet.	❑	❑
Notify people key to the nonprofit.	❑	❑
Tell volunteers and clients about changes in services/operations.	❑	❑
Respond to media.	❑	❑
Keep a media log of callers and questions.	❑	❑
Update media as situation develops.	❑	❑
Follow up implications; prevent backlash.	❑	❑
Evaluate and tweak the system.	❑	❑
Other _____	❑	❑
Other _____	❑	❑

Crisis Activities Log

Name of Nonprofit _____

Describe Crisis (who, what, when, where, why?) _____

_____

_____

Date   Time   Action / By whom?

_____ _____   _____

_____ _____   _____

_____ _____   _____

_____ _____   _____

Self-assessment Worksheet

(Crisis Response Team)

This worksheet can be completed as a group effort by the team working together, or individually by each team member.

What Happened? _____

Major Causes? _____

Time Line (recognition to response to end) _____

How soon was the board informed about the crisis?

❑ within hours   ❑ within 24 hours   ❑ within a week   ❑ never, because _____

Did the media learn of the crisis? ❑ Yes   ❑ No How? _____

How effectively did the organization respond to media inquiries?

❑ very effectively   ❑ somewhat effectively   ❑ ineffectively

How effective was the crisis response team?

❑ highly effective   ❑ effective   ❑ marginally effective

What, if any, skills or talents were missing in the make-up of the team?

Did the team follow the action plan? If not, what were the deviations and why? Should these deviations be incorporated into a revised plan?

Did the plan work? What could be done more effectively/efficiently and how?

Does the plan need to be changed in other ways? How?

Was prompt contact made with outside resources, such as police, fire, ambulance, insurance companies, lawyers and those whose help was needed during the crisis?

Additional Publications Available from the
Nonprofit Risk Management Center
www.nonprofitrisk.org

Full Speed Ahead: Managing Technology Risk in the Nonprofit World

No matter how large or small your technological advances, they are critical to your mission. This book will help you protect your people, financial and property assets, whether you have two PCs networked together or a multisystem network at remote locations. *Full Speed Ahead* addresses how the wired and wireless worlds affect employment practices, staffing plans, volunteer recruitment, fund-raising, crisis management, copyright, security, privacy and confidentiality, client protection and insurance coverage. 2001 / 120 pages / $25.00

No Surprises: Harmonizing Risk and Reward in Volunteer Management — *2nd Edition*

This second edition of the popular *No Surprises* is a clear, easy-to-read guide that demystifies "risk management" and explains this responsibility of every director of volunteers in any type of setting. Learn how to limit risk at each step of managing a volunteer program: in volunteer job design, the application and screening process, and ongoing training and supervision. This expanded edition includes privacy and technology risk reduction methods. 2001 / 95 pages / $15.00

Mission Accomplished: A Practical Guide to Risk Management for Nonprofits — *2nd Edition*

This valuable book explains why risk management is an essential tool in achieving a nonprofit's mission. It removes the mystique surrounding risk management and provides practical advice on how to establish an effective risk management program. *Mission Accomplished* explains the risk management process and discusses several special risk categories. *The second edition features a new section on information age risks.* 1999 / 78 pages / $25.00

No Strings Attached: Managing the Risks of Fundraising & Collaboration

This publications provides a practical framework through which nonprofit CEOs, boards, and others engaged in fundraising can address the risks and pursue fundraising responsibly. The authors address the risks associated with budgeting, raising money from foundations, soliciting individual donors, obtaining corporate support, negotiating collaborations and partnerships, and the challenge of restricted funding. 1999 / 95 pages / $15.00

Taking the High Road: A Guide to Effective and Legal Employment Practices for Nonprofits

This book is the first comprehensive guide to employment risk management for nonprofits. You will learn how to do the right thing, comply with the law, and stay out of trouble. Topics addressed in the book include avoiding illegal discrimination, complying with the ADA, developing a CEO contract, updating an employee handbook, conducting drug testing, complying with family and medical leave laws and safe reference-giving practices. 1999 / 217 pages / $45.00

The Best Defense: 10 Steps to Surviving a Lawsuit

This book is a must-have for nonprofit CEOs, execs and board members. The text describes 10 steps to help a nonprofit survive litigation with minimal damage to morale, reputation, and the ability to focus on mission-critical activities. Chapters focus on working with your insurer, communicating with constituencies, understanding the process, minding the time clock, and much much more. 1998 / 54 pages / $12.00

D&O: What You Need to Know

This resource on nonprofit directors' and officers' liability insurance describes important subtleties in nonprofit D&O coverage. If you're considering the first-time purchase of D&O coverage or you want to make sure that your current policy provides the coverage you need, this book will be invaluable. The text outlines risk management strategies for governance risks, provides an overview of the emergence of nonprofit D&O coverage, and offers useful insight on the D&O application, coverage elements, and policy nuances. The book concludes with tips on reading an insurance policy, purchasing coverage, and answers to frequently asked questions about nonprofit D&O insurance. 1998 / 60 pages / $15.00

Leaving Nothing to Chance: Achieving Board Accountability Through Risk Management

Risk management plays a fundamental role in the governance of a nonprofit, and every board is both responsible for the overall well-being of the organization and accountable to its constituencies. This booklet outlines 10 steps for achieving board accountability through risk management, including formulating risk management policies, creating models for safe volunteer and staff activities, organizing a risk management committee, establishing sound financial management policies, ensuring proper management of the board's activities and seeking expert help from trustworthy sources. 1998 / 34 pages / $12.00

More Than a Matter of Trust: Managing the Risks of Mentoring

All social service programs face risks, but the elements of trust and personal relationships dramatically raise the stakes for mentoring programs. This book will help you develop a solid risk management plan for your mentoring program that will help you protect your mentees, your mentors and your organization's assets — including its good name. *More Than a Matter of Trust* explains the legal liabilities that mentoring programs face and shows you how to develop a risk management plan by presenting "10 Keys to Mentoring Risk Management. 1998 / 59 pages / $15.00

Staff Screening Tool Kit: Building a Strong Foundation Through Careful Staffing — 2nd Edition

During the past four years, several thousand nonprofit and other organizations have used the first edition of the *Staff Screening Tool Kit* for guidance on effective screening. Since the original *Tool Kit* was first published, changes have taken place that influence the screening process and govern access to records. Besides these issues, the second edition addresses the increased focus on official agency records as tools for staff screening, and features a state-by-state directory of agencies that maintain records useful for screening. 1998 / 135 pages / $30.00

Managing Special Event Risks: Ten Steps to Safety

Published by the Nonprofit Risk Management Center and Nonprofits' Insurance Alliance of California, this guide provides tips on controlling the risks associated with special events. Topics include goal setting, identification and evaluation of risks, risk sharing and transfer, emergency procedures, event documentation, and working with the media. Checklists and forms are included in the appendix. 1997 / 60 pages / $12.00

To see a complete listing of available publications,

visit www.nonprofitrisk.org.

To place an order, visit our Web site or call (202) 785-3891, today.

Notes